' Co

The Strategic Planning Workbook

THIRD EDITION

The Strategic Planning Workbook

Neville Lake

KoganPage

LONDON PHILADELPHIA NEW DELHI

First published in Great Britain in 2002
Second edition published in Great Britain and the United States in 2006 by Kogan Page Limited
Third edition 2012

120 Pentonville Road
London N1 9JN
United Kingdom
www.koganpage.com

1518 Walnut Street, Suite 1100
Philadelphia PA 19102
USA

4737/23 Ansari Road
Daryaganj
New Delhi 110002
India

© Neville Lake, 2002, 2006, 2012

The right of Neville Lake to be identified as the author of this work has been asserted by him in accordance with the Copyright, Designs and Patents Act 1988.

ISBN   978 0 7494 6500 1
E-ISBN   978 0 7494 6501 8

British Library Cataloguing-in-Publication Data

A CIP record for this book is available from the British Library.

Library of Congress Cataloging-in-Publication Data

Lake, Neville.
   The strategic planning workbook / Neville Lake. – 3rd ed.
      p. cm.
   Includes index.
   ISBN 978-0-7494-6500-1 – ISBN 978-0-7494-6501-8 (ebook)   1. Strategic planning.   I. Title.
   HD30.28.L35 2012
   658.4'012–dc23
                                                                                          2011047305

Typeset by Graphicraft Ltd, Hong Kong
Printed and bound in India by Replika Press Pvt Ltd

CONTENTS

Video material to support this book is available at the Kogan Page website:
www.koganpage.com/editions/the-strategic-planning-workbook/9780749465001

PREFACE

Strategy. It's a great word, isn't it? Just put the word 'strategic' in front of a project and it shines a little brighter than all others. Look at the funding for activities – those that are labelled 'strategic' get the largest slice. The CEO's projects are almost always 'strategic projects', and these – and all the others that go by the same name – get first priority. But what is a strategic project? Indeed, what is strategy?

This is a surprisingly difficult question to answer, because 'strategy' is a term that means different things to different people, and too often it becomes a business process that hinders rather than helps organizations to take control of their future. It is difficult to get a good definition of strategy because:

- Too many strategists focus on the grandest strategic dilemmas. They write about how to shape a new business to take advantage of a breakthrough market opportunity. These are serious and real challenges. However, they trouble mid-sized and small businesses extremely infrequently, and only occasionally affect large multinationals.

- Many of the texts ignore the fact that there are boundaries for most organizations. The typical business is caught in a web of past financial commitments, current competencies and future contracts. The problem is not to seek new places to do business, but rather to take the greatest advantage of current opportunities.

- While there are boundaries, the amount of freedom you have within your available options is too often underestimated. Strategy is as much about choice as it is about analysis. I have found that those organizations that dream the big dream, pick the seemingly unattainable goal but also develop a great strategy are the ones that end up dominating their industry. If you ask the questions 'Where do we want to be?' and 'What do we have to do to get there?' and then have the courage to do what it takes, then success is likely to be the result. Most writers do not appreciate the blending of art, science, passion and performance that makes a good strategy.

- Most strategy books are interesting but leave you no closer to being able to complete a strategic planning project at a practical level. They present strategy as a theoretical pursuit, rather than a way to make practical decisions.

The consequence is that the definition of 'strategy' is overburdened by grand models put forward by theorists for multinationals. The average organization is left with an understanding of 'strategy' that is distorted and impractical.

Strategy should be about thinking clearly and acting deliberately, so that you can get the most out of your current and potential opportunities. This book provides you with the concepts you need to perform this thinking, the tools you need to gather the necessary information, the techniques you require to make decisions and the frameworks to translate your conclusions into practical action plans. When you have completed the exercises, data gathering, analysis, the two workshops and the implementation plan, you will have a map to your best future possible.

This book uses a practical definition of strategic planning, as follows:

> Strategic planning is gaining insights about where you are now, gathering the information that identifies where you should be in the future, generating the decisions that will give you a unique position, and then defining the actions that will bridge the gap.

Strategic implementation is defined as:

> The ongoing application of those decisions and actions so that the outcomes are achieved.

This is a book that has been designed for managers who own/work for organizations that are already established. It has been written in the expectation that, if you are reading this, you are the person responsible in your organization for making strategic planning happen, which means that you are the CEO, you are in planning/finance... or you were away when the other members of the management team voted on who should do this year's strategic plan.

This book is practical, eclectic and pragmatic – it gets the job done. The tools provided in this book are a mixture of my own diagnostic and analytical techniques and decision-making processes, along with many of the strategic planning standards and favourites.

The book is written to show you how to generate good information for decision making, without expecting you to take a couple of months off to find the data. The exercises show you how to make the kinds of practical decisions that enable you to build on your past, so that you can secure success in the future. The workshops show you how to go about identifying what practical strategy means for you in your organization – whether it is large or small.

The book applies if you own the organization, run it, or manage a bit of it. In the book I have considered customers as people/organizations that pay money for your products or services. However, many of the same concepts

ACKNOWLEDGEMENTS

It is not easy writing a book, particularly when your office is attached to your home.

I am fortunate that I have been blessed with a wife – and business partner – who understands when I would welcome a distraction and when I need to be left alone, who knows when to give me a push and when to rein in my enthusiasm, and who has been an excellent editor and constructive critic of all the drafts. So, Gayle, thank you for living through yet another edition with me.

I would also like to thank all the people who have guided my development as a strategist, and all the clients who have rewarded my involvement in their strategic processes with so much effort and enthusiasm. In particular I would like to thank Geof Johns, who is a great strategic thinker and constantly challenges me to try a little harder and reach a little further.

Turning a manuscript into a book is no small task. I would like to thank Pauline Goodwin for starting the ball rolling, and Jon Finch who oversaw the production of the first two editions. I would particularly like to thank Nicola de Jong who provided fresh ideas and a new framework for this edition as well as managing all the steps that have brought it into your hands.

I would also like to thank Roy Stanton for working with me to film the 40-minute video about the strategic retreat that accompanies this book (see Kogan Page website).

ABOUT THE AUTHOR

Neville Lake is a Registered Psychologist, an internationally recognized strategic planner and a business improvement specialist (which is an unusual – possibly unique – combination). He has worked for three of the world's largest consulting firms, written seven books, visited over 100 best-practice organizations, consulted to over 150 businesses and has been applauded by over 500,000 people in countries across the world. He established his own business, The Lake Group, in 1998.

Neville has developed his understanding of how businesses work through visits to world best-practice organizations, including British Airways, Cadbury Schweppes, Citibank, Disneyland, Federal Express, Harrods, Mars, NASA, Ritz-Carlton, Rolls-Royce, Shell, Starbucks and Wrigley's. The knowledge he has collected, and the wisdom he has achieved, has been applied in strategic planning assignments with leading organizations.

Neville specializes in facilitating strategic retreats, and has helped organizations to: a) clearly define what they should become; b) map a pathway to achieve those goals; and c) develop and implement a detailed and practical action plan. Neville has also helped to reshape divisional performance, revitalized processes (such as customer service), designed business transformation and coached senior managers. He has worked with clients in locations around the world, including Australia, China, Europe, Hong Kong, India, Indonesia, Malaysia, New Zealand, Saudi Arabia, United Arab Emirates (Dubai), the United Kingdom and the United States.

A powerful, entertaining and informative speaker, Neville blends facts with examples, stories with case studies, and ideas with implementation strategies; he delivers profound messages with a light touch and plenty of humour. He has featured in a BBC documentary, spoken on radio, appeared in the press and written many articles.

His other books include the forthcoming *Practical Strategy* (aimed at the busy manager who is looking to put together a powerful plan in a short space of time, this new title will complement *The Strategic Planning Workbook*), *The Customer Service Workbook*, the best-selling *The Third*

Principle: How to get 20% more out of your business, and *The Greatest Planet in the Universe*.

Neville has developed unique diagnostic tools that reveal unseen business opportunities. He asks questions that compel people to examine how they gain results and provides the techniques and inspiration to help people to renew their businesses.

Please visit Neville at: **www.lakegroup.com.au** for free videos and articles.

Getting a bigger brain

How to think like a strategist

The business wasn't doing well.

Sure, every year it made more than the year before. But that wasn't the point. With the customer contacts, position in the market, accumulated knowledge and intellectual property that they had, Malcolm knew that this business was maybe half of what it could be – or should be. He knew that if he could really focus all the resources in the business on those opportunities that would deliver the greatest benefits, the sky would be the limit.

In three months he was scheduled to lead a 'strategic retreat' with the senior management team. They had done these before, with the same result: a tedious repetition of each person's ambitions for the future followed by some scrappy action planning. Then it was all forgotten a month later. If he was honest, the best part had been the dinner.

This time it would be different. This time he would force the group to 'think strategically'.

Malcolm is right. All strategy starts with strategic thinking.

Strategic thinking is not the same as strategic planning. Strategic thinking involves stepping back from your organization so that you can view it in a way that helps you to understand what is important today, and what you need to do to make it successful in the future.

Strategic thinking is different from the kind of thinking that you do every day. For example, sketch your organization on a piece of paper. Draw the people (as matchstick figures if you need to – no one is going to see it), the premises, the bits of equipment that you use and the customers who are the lucky recipients of your outputs. Briefly list what people do, and what customers get.

Now draw another picture that shows how and where value is created for you and your customers, where the greatest areas of opportunity and the weakest links are, where there is untapped potential, where there is over-investment, where you are trapped by past decisions, and where you have the most direct path to increased profits. This is not such an easy picture to draw.

The second picture is a challenge because we typically think about our organizations in terms of what we do, not in terms of where the value is hiding or what we could be doing instead. You need a different approach. This is what strategic thinking is all about.

Contrary to popular belief, strategic thinking is not rocket science. It simply requires that you collect different data and use the right models to help you understand what really happens in your organization, and where the possibilities reside. It is a viewpoint that you will develop as you read this book.

By the time you complete all the chapters you will see your organization in terms of value, and what you need to do to deliver that value. You will be able to recognize sub-optimization and see opportunities. As you progress through the exercises you will learn how to gather the data that you need and how to apply the models that will make sense of that data. You can then achieve the future that you want, the returns that your shareholders deserve, and opportunities that your employees expect.

By the time you get to the end of this book you will wish that you had been familiar with strategic thinking right from the start. This chapter is designed to get the right kind of thinking started now. Consider it as the essential warm-up before the main event.

Strategic thinking can be summarized by three sets of four questions.

1. The really big questions

- What business are we in?
- What is possible for this business?
- What is our uniqueness?
- What is important to our success?

2. The key tactical questions

- When do we create value for our customers and for ourselves?
- Where are the areas of greatest opportunity?
- How much money do we want to make?
- What do we have to do to sustain optimal levels of performance?

3. The true operational questions

- What needs to be done?
- What gets priority?
- Who will do this and by when?
- What is the best way to complete the steps?

Within these questions are the insights that will help you to make sense of your organization today and that will lead you to develop it into the organization that it needs to be tomorrow.

In this chapter I have covered the big questions and the tactical questions, so that you have a strategic and tactical perspective before you start to gather the data. The operational questions are not described in detail here. These are embedded in the action planning activities described in this book. The other parts of the book are written so that you can collect information with others or lead discussions. This part is written primarily for you – to be enjoyed on your own to prepare you for all that is to come.

The really big questions

What business are we in?

There are three parts to this question: What business are we in now?, What business are we not in? What business should we be in?

What business are we in now?

There are typically two answers to this question. The first one is 'Duh, that's obvious. We do... (whatever your business describes itself to be on your website)', and the second answer – which is a real description of the business.

The reason that there are two answers is that business terms are imprecise. If you were to collect up a bundle of organizations that all apparently did the same thing and pull each apart, the chances are that you would find that each had a different emphasis, each had different customers and each had different kinds of products/services. There could well be some that were so different that they were really in a different business altogether.

The problem is that an organization starts by using a label of some sort (white goods manufacturer, law firm, supermarket and so on). The label used is imprecise, and means different things to different people. This organization then evolves by small increments over time. Individuals still apply the label, and think of themselves as belonging to that kind of organization without seriously challenging what that label means, or checking if the label still applies.

A quick way to find out what business you are in is to independently ask three senior people to describe what the organization does, and which customers are the beneficiaries of these efforts. These three people are not allowed to use any labels or commonly accepted descriptions of organizations.

Then ask three 'why' questions – which quite simply means asking the question 'why' to the answer given, three times ('to make money' is not the answer at this point – it is too broad). The persistent use of 'why' (you can ask it five times if you think that you can get away without it being too irritating) forces people to get back to key issues. The chances are that you will have different answers from each person.

TABLE 1.1   'Why?' questions

What we do and who the customer is	Why?	Why?	Why?
Person 1			
Person 2			
Person 3			

The shock value of this little exercise gives you the impetus to extend the questioning to more people. Keep asking the same questions until you get no new answers. Then list all the different responses, using Table 1.1. Now, lump together those responses that broadly describe the same activities and outcomes for the same customers; use Table 1.2.

TABLE 1.2   Common activities/outcomes, customers and reasons

Common activities/outcomes (what)	Common customers (who)	Common reasons (third why)

Then rank order the items on your list in Table 1.3 by how often people picked that definition of your organization.

TABLE 1.3   What, who and why

Rank order	What	Who	Why
1			
2			
3			
4			
5			
6			
7			
8			
9			
and so on			

This is what you really do – right now. It may be an untidy description – the what, who and why may not perfectly line up (which tells you something), but it is an interesting snapshot. It is probably different from the way that you describe your organization on your website.

A more scientific, but longer, way to get to the same end point is to briefly analyse the different business segments that are covered by your organization (do not invest too much time here, you will complete a detailed analysis later on).

A segment exists when you can identify:

- a set of activities/products/services that are clearly different from each other;
- different customers who receive the same product/service;
- a defined geographic region with a set of customers who consistently buy your products and services.

List all the possible segments that you have and then rank these by value to your business; see Table 1.4.

TABLE 1.4   Segments by product, customer and geographic region

Segments by product	
Segment	Rank order
	1
	2
	3
	4
	5
Segments by customer	
Segment	Rank order
	1
	2
	3
	4
	5
Segments by geographic region	
Segment	Rank order
	1
	2
	3
	4
	5

The chances are that the first few items at the top of the list represent the bulk of the value in your organization. Typically the Pareto principle (the 80:20 rule) will be at work – you will find that 80 per cent of the value delivered to your organization comes from only 20 per cent of the items on the list. This is the business that you are in. It may have no logic to it, it may make no sense, it may not fit under any commonly accepted label – but this is it.

What business are we not in?

This is another face of the question about the nature of the business that you are in. It is a question in its own right, and the answer is particularly important.

The decision not to develop in a particular direction, not to challenge specific competitors, and not to offer certain products/services places boundaries around your organization. The trouble is that too often decisions taken in the past (in response to the circumstances of the day) are never properly reviewed. In this way the past keeps on influencing the present – and possibly denying you a future.

For the moment, at the beginning of the strategic process, consider these questions:

- What decisions has your organization taken that exclude you from pursuing opportunities?
- What could your organization be doing (with the available resources that are within the skills of the existing people) if some of those decisions were reversed?
- Are there real opportunities for your organization if those restrictions were lifted?
- Why are you not taking advantage of these opportunities?
- Is it possible that if some of the boundaries were lifted, you would be able to develop your organization with little extra investment in resources?

These questions may suggest that you need to free your business from the cumulative effect of too many past restrictions. That is an interesting piece of information to have at the beginning of your strategic process, and can be noted down. However, also consider that too few limitations also create their own set of problems.

If there are few restrictions in your organization, then it may have been driven by the personal preferences and passions of the managers who have been in positions of influence over the years. In this case lots of forays into different markets will probably have left a legacy of a multitude of marginally successful products in different segments, which have the combined effect of soaking up management attention and weakening your business. You will see this in the analysis of segments. If there are many small (not particularly profitable) segments, then you are probably the victim of insufficient boundaries around the business. To capture this thinking, complete the gains and drains table.

TABLE 1.5   Possible gains and drains

Possible gains		
	Why is this currently 'off limits?'	Possible value
1		
2		
3		
4		
5		
Possible drains		
	Why has this evolved?	Possible cost
1		
2		
3		
4		
5		

What business should we be in?

Your challenge is to match your capabilities with the opportunities. You have a jumble of opportunities available (some are promising, and some are not worth the effort) and these represent your 'circle of opportunity'; see Figure 1.1. Most businesses have a limited quantity of resources (people's time and money) and virtually unlimited opportunities. The trick is to concentrate your resources on those opportunities that will sustainably deliver the greatest amount of value to your business. There is a place in your 'circle of opportunity' that is exactly right for your business.

FIGURE 1.1   The circle of opportunity

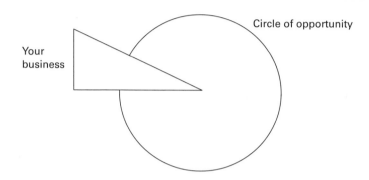

Think carefully about this picture. It is the summary of all that you will be doing in this strategic planning process. As you progress through this book you will be looking for the places where the areas of greatest opportunity reside, where your uniqueness is centred and where you will find the resources that you will need to achieve your best possible future.

For now, consider your current situation. Your organization already has a trajectory into the future, and a momentum that is carrying it forward. If you do nothing, then you will carry on in much the same direction. Ask yourself the following questions:

- If we change nothing, what kind of business will we become?
- Is this where there are the best opportunities for us?
- If this is not the kind of business that we want to be, what is a better alternative?
- Do we have the resources to become this alternative?

These questions may be difficult to answer, and may be troubling. They should be. You are not ready to fully answer these questions now – at the beginning of the process – but keep them on a piece of paper and refer to them often as you gather and interpret the information that you will collect as you progress through this book.

What is possible for this business?

As you progress through this book – and through the strategic planning process – one of the most important questions that you will struggle to answer is 'What is possible for this business?' You will return to this question several times in your strategic journey, and to help you to process it successfully keep in mind that there are really only four choices:

1 Stay the same, and get better (improve).

2 Stay the same, and get bigger (replicate).

3 Keep some parts the same, and introduce parts that are different (evolve).

4 Become substantially different (reinvent).

FIGURE 1.2   Four choices

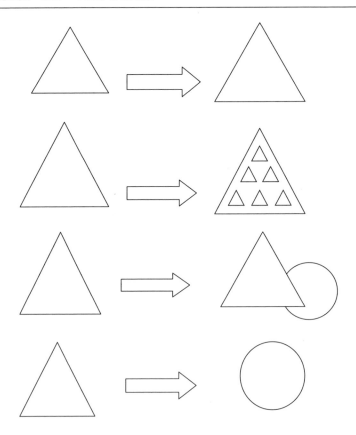

1. Stay the same, and get better

Few businesses can stay exactly the same. New technology, competitive pressures, customer opportunities and so on will compel you to change. However, there are a few that can – and will – stay much the same. At one end of the scale these types of businesses could be small, unique, in a niche market and able to produce stunning profits for their owners, or at the other end, they could be organizations that have boundaries imposed. Some public sector or public-sector type organizations fall into this category.

2. Stay the same, and get bigger

Some businesses become larger versions of themselves. Where they currently produce 1,000 units for sale, they will produce 10,000 units, or where they once served 100 customers, they now serve 1,000 customers. For example, these are the chain stores or franchises where more and more identical units are added on. Now of course scale adds complexity, so they also have to get better, but the basic business model is one of replication rather than reinvention.

3. Keep some parts the same, and introduce parts that are different

This choice is right for organizations that have enough competency and cash to take advantage of a new market or technology. This foray into something new may be achieved for different reasons and in a number of different ways; for example, a) reducing uncertainty or costs by acquiring a supplier, b) opening new doors and reducing costs through merging with a competitor, c) leveraging customer relationships by developing compatible but different products or services.

4. Become substantially different

This is often a 'bet the business' choice if it applies to a large portion of the organization, or 'bet my job' if it is focused on a narrower section. This is the choice for those organizations that are really in the wrong spot in their circle of opportunity and have to make some big changes or go to the wall.

Of course, these are not 'either/or' choices that apply to the whole business. It may be that different parts of your business will receive different treatment, and it is important that you are crystal clear about which choice is in play.

For the moment, consider the key parts of your business over the next five years and place them in Table 1.6.

TABLE 1.6 Categorizing the key parts of your business according to the four choices

	Which part should receive this treatment?	Why?	What are the implications?	What could this be worth (in $)?
Improve				
Replicate				
Evolve				
Reinvent				

The final column helps you to make an initial assessment of 'what is possible'. If you have enough information you could complete the same table again, but this time with a 10–15-year horizon.

What is our uniqueness?

It was a tough decision. There were several proposals, and they were all around the same price. James was in charge of the tendering process, and he knew more about the hopefuls than everyone else. He was getting a real grilling from the selection panel.

The question he had just been asked was 'So, what makes this business different? It seems to offer the same as the others, but has nothing particularly special.'

James thought hard. The answer came to him. 'Nothing,' he replied. The panel put that proposal to one side.

If you own, or know, or can do something that no one else can readily replicate then you have an edge. If customers value what makes you unique, then you are going to be busy. If large numbers of customers are willing to pay a premium for whatever you have that makes you unique – then you are going to be rich.

Ask five people in your organization what delivers your uniqueness. Ask five customers the same question. If you get different answers then you have not properly identified and articulated what gives you a special place. If you have identified no particular uniqueness at this stage, then as you progress through the strategic planning process you should be looking for information that suggests where this might lie. As the data comes to light ask yourself two questions: 'What is the most likely source of our uniqueness?' and 'What would we have to do to develop and/or sustain that uniqueness?'

If you are able to identify where you have uniqueness then ask the follow-up questions: 'In what way does the customer value this uniqueness?' and 'In what way does this uniqueness help us to make money?'

In what way does the customer value this uniqueness?

Having uniqueness and making sure that your customers understand and appreciate that uniqueness do not necessarily happen together. There are plenty of electronic products, computers and car engines that have a unique feature which is so exciting to the designers that it keeps them awake at night – but is of the utmost irrelevance to the customer.

A good way to focus your thinking is to consider the well-used distinction between features, advantages and benefits (FAB analysis). This has been a standard in the advertising industry for many years, and is a practical way to help organizations to see what they do from the point of view of the recipient. The definitions for each are:

- Features are the characteristics of the product/service.
- Advantages are those aspects of the product/service that are in some way different from the competitors'.
- Benefits are the value that the customer gains from using the product/service (and are often about money and time).

So, to take a straightforward example, the writing style for this book would have the following FAB analysis:

- Features – is written in an accessible style.
- Advantages – the analyses and exercises are easy to follow.
- Benefits – you can quickly identify how to improve profit and 'strategic strength'.

The trick in progressing from one to the next is to identify a feature and then add the words 'which means that' until you find an advantage and then a benefit. Again, using the book example, the FAB analysis written as a sentence is as follows: 'The book is written in an accessible style, which means that the analyses and exercises are easy to follow, which means that you can quickly identify how to improve profit and strategic strength.'

The customer (in this case, you) can assess this book against others. As the competition is not advertising their books as helping you to 'quickly identify how to improve profit and strategic strength', then this book has a uniqueness which makes it attractive.

Try this with one of your products and/or services, using Table 1.7.

TABLE 1.7   Features, advantages and benefits (FABs) of a key product/service

Key product	Feature:
	Advantage:
	Benefit:
Key service	Feature:
	Advantage:
	Benefit:

With the distinction between features, advantages and benefits in mind, think clearly about your uniqueness from your customers' point of view. Imagine that you have bought a full page of advertising space in the magazine that is read by most of your customers. You are going to write one sentence in the middle of the page that punches out the message about your organization's uniqueness. What would you write in Table 1.8?

TABLE 1.8   Uniqueness of your product/service

Our product/service is unique because...

This is good for you because...

You really need this product/service because...

If you have no crisp answer to this question now, then make sure that you collect enough data to easily provide the answer by the completion of the strategic planning process.

In what way does this uniqueness help us make money?

If you found a good, strong statement for your uniqueness, then it will be relatively obvious how you can use this to make money. However, in some cases the uniqueness you have may not be particularly exciting to the customer, but it enables you to deliver products/services at a high quality and low cost.

If this kind of uniqueness applies to your business, then complete the same kind of exercise, with Table 1.9, and imagine that you are still going to write the one sentence for a magazine – except this time it is one that only shareholders will read. The sentence that you create will be about the special bottom-line advantage of your uniqueness. This will not necessarily be shared with customers, but it will appear where it is required to shape decisions within your organization. Again, make sure that you collect the data to enable you to answer this question during the strategic process.

TABLE 1.9   Uniqueness of your organization

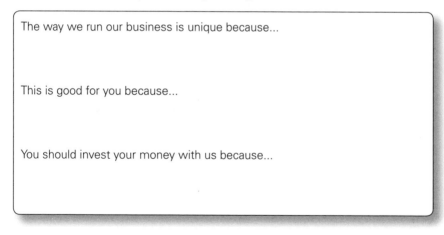

The way we run our business is unique because...

This is good for you because...

You should invest your money with us because...

Developing a clear statement of uniqueness is not easy. If you cannot find one at the moment do not despair; it is early days in the strategic planning process. It is also worth bearing in mind that while most businesses have some form of uniqueness, this is not true of all. If it turns out that you do not have uniqueness, and there seems to be no easy way to develop it, then it does not mean that your organization has no legitimate place, nor does it mean that you will not be able to operate profitably. A lack of uniqueness is manageable if you are the kind of organization that is in the relationship with your competitors where you are 'in the waiting room', or better still 'trawling' in a large pool of customers (see the comments about competitors in Chapter 2). In these cases there is plenty of demand, and if the supply of businesses able to meet that demand comprises many small players, then everyone has the chance to make a profit. But beware: there is a danger that large players will develop to take a big slice of the market – and maybe your business.

What is important to our success?

The greatest influence exerted by managers is where they place their attention. If your measures are about financial performance, if all the management meetings are about financial performance, and if all the reports that are generated are about financial performance, then the focus of all the managers in your organization is going to be about (guess what) financial performance.

What you define as important, and how this importance is embodied in your measurement systems, are perhaps the most powerful of all strategic messages, and drive everyday performance. Where do you think something like a customer service programme, or a human resource change, or a programme to develop and sustain 'respect' will sit in an organization that is totally financially driven? That's right, at the bottom of everyone's in-tray – no matter how often people say that these programmes are important.

The secret to working out what is really important is not to listen to the rhetoric. It is easy to put together a few slogans, and they are quickly forgotten. Rather, look at what kind of information is gathered and how this is used to fuel the measures. People know that what gets measured gets attended to, and everything else can wait – perhaps forever. Consider these questions:

- What kinds of information do you gather about organizational performance?
- What do the bulk of your measures cover?
- What do you spend most time talking about at management meetings?
- What do people infer is important from where you invest your attention?
- How does this perception drive the way that they emphasize and complete their work?

It is probable that most of the attention is directed towards financial performance, and it is likely that most of the financial information is about what happened in the past, not what is likely to happen next (which is why we are not practised at predicting the future). Consider the implications of the messages you are sending to the people in your business by where you put your attention; and toy with the idea that a change in focus will be amplified throughout your organization.

Now, think about your organization in a different way. Think about what really drives success today.

Try this simple experiment. Find a tall building in a large town/city. Stand at street level and concentrate on the experience. Be aware of the buzz of the traffic, the blur of people rushing by, the smell of machinery and buildings, the effect of the weather conditions. Now, travel in the lift to the executive floor at the top of the building, and look out of the CEO's window. You could be on another planet. Your surroundings are quiet, unhurried, and sanitized by air conditioning. You can see the clean edges of the surrounding office blocks with their gleaming cliffs of windows, the hills in the distance and the sky above. The individual people and the traffic are tiny and insignificant.

Too many organizations have a picture of the business that is like the view out of the CEO's window. Up here aggregated figures represent activities, numbers of employees replace individual names, trend information about customer preferences takes the place of gut instinct, and relentless waves of financial data feed mathematical models that are supposed to show if the organization is still on track.

The most common mistake organizations make is to think that this view of the organization is the real engine room of current profit and future success. It isn't. It is a shadow. This thinking has robbed many businesses of their future, it has cost many shareholders a lot of money, and it has cut short many promising careers.

The profit tree, shown in Figure 1.3, is a powerful way to highlight those places in your business that truly make a difference. This shows how an organization really works. Essentially, this model shows that profit – in the box on the right – is a blunt measure. Profit is the consequence of properly managing a number of 'profit drivers'. These profit drivers (typically from four to six of them in most organizations) are in turn made up from a set of 'key activities' (maybe 20 to 40 in total). It is at the activity level that real control is exerted. Make a list of what these are in your business.

FIGURE 1.3   The profit tree

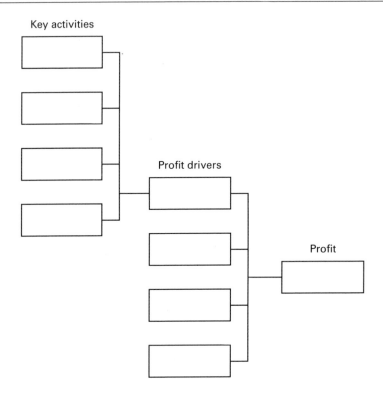

You can now see the 20 to 40 key activities that deliver profits to your organization. These are activities that you can control. This is where you should have the key measures for your organization, and it is these activities that senior managers should talk about with front-line employees. Take a look at your current measures. How many of the key activities are made important by a significant measure? How many are currently left out all together?

Two outcomes immediately flow when senior executives start to talk about the activities at this level. The first is that they connect with managers and front-line people. Now the people at the top are talking about activities that they recognize (not the more general concept of profit, which they do not). Secondly, by specifying what they want to happen at the activity level, those at the front line know what they have to do, and can respond in a way that delivers the intended outcome. When you put together the implementation plans in Chapter 8, you need to make sure that the outcomes you want are delivered by activities that are properly measured using a profit tree.

So, you have now covered the big questions. At the beginning of the process these questions will serve to make you think about your organization. These big questions will raise more questions and they will direct your attention to the kinds of data that you need to gather. Towards the conclusion of the process (in the decision-making workshop) these big questions will surface again to help you to find the answers that will define your business and focus attention.

The key tactical questions

The key tactical questions are answered by the data that you will gather as you complete the exercises in this book. To help you make sense of the data as you collect it, keep the following questions in mind. You will cover some of this ground again later in the book, and when you do it will make a lot more sense because you will have started the right thinking on these pages.

When do we create value for our customers and for ourselves?

> Brian looked out of his office door. He could see the usual shuffle of activity. People were carrying bits of paper around, they were in little knots talking to each other, and the meeting rooms were full. There was so much to do, and Brian had another request from the supervisors for extra staff. He had no choice – if he wanted to get the work done he needed the people.

Every day people complete thousands of activities in your organization, probably tens of thousands. When you walk through your organization everyone is busy. The fact that everyone is always busy has nothing to do with the amount of work that actually needs to be done. What fills people's days is a jumble of activities that truly make a contribution and those that – to be brutally honest – need not have been completed at all. The trouble is that it is difficult to tell the difference.

The problem is that work grows like weeds. Think about what would happen if you took an average employee, put him or her in an office with a desk and a phone – and then left him or her alone. No instructions, no tasks. Then you came back in six months' time. You would find that the person had phone calls to return, meetings to attend, travel requisitions for you to authorize. He or she would have found 'work'.

To get a rough picture of how much real work is being completed in your organization, imagine that you have three different coloured 'Post-it' notes. Imagine that you could stick yellow notes on those activities that create value for your customers, blue notes on all those activities that create value for your organization, and red notes on those activities that do not make much difference to either. How much red are you going to see?

The chances are that there will be between 20 and 40 per cent of what is going on in your organization that will attract a red sticker. (If you are interested in this, then there is more in my book, *The Third Principle – How to get 20% more out of your business*, which is available through **www.lakegroup.com.au**.)

You will find it easier to centre your activities on those that you want to retain if you keep clearly in mind that the purpose of every organization is to create value for itself and its customers. To create value for your customers you need to be absolutely sure what makes a difference to them, and you need to continually monitor changes in their needs, wants and expectations. You also need to be sure what they are able to get from your competitors, and why they might take their business elsewhere.

To create value for yourself you need to be clear about how to complete the necessary activities in the best way possible. This means having a clear understanding of all the processes, and having ways to refine those processes so that they work in the optimum way.

There are many other activities that will creep into any organization. There will be plenty in yours right now. All those red activities – sapping your time and draining your resources. The more of these you carry, the less competitive you will be. Use the data that you will gather in Chapters 2 and 3 to identify where value is created and destroyed in your organization.

Where are the areas of greatest opportunity?

Think about a huge supermarket. You can pick whatever you want from any shelf, but you can only have a limited number of items in your shopping trolley at any one time. You can only put a new item in when you take an existing item out. You need to make sure that the basket always contains those items that you value the most. Life is like that – the search for the best set of choices from an almost infinite set of options.

Your organization is like that too. The trick is to identify those options that will deliver the best of outcomes and the greatest amount of profit to your organization with the least amount of effort, both now and in the future.

The chances are that some of your time and activities today are not centred in this zone. You need to stop investing in these as soon as possible.

It is also highly likely that you are not taking advantage of some of the opportunities that are naturally yours in the marketplace. You need to rapidly start to capture these opportunities before someone else does.

Many of the diagnostics that we will use in the next two chapters will help you to identify these, but for now – as you get yourself oriented towards thinking tactically – consider these questions:

- Which processes generate the most value in your organization right now?
- Which processes are likely to generate the most value in the future?
- Which products/services generate the most profit now?
- Which products/services are likely to generate the most profit in the future?
- Which customers give you the greatest return now?
- Which customers are likely to give you the greatest return in the future?
- Which customers waste your time and money?
- Where is there greater capacity to do more work with high-return customers?
- Where are there more of the kinds of customers that you would like?

Most organizations can recognize relatively quickly where value is generated and can list a bundle of customers that they should not have, and identify those that they should.

How much money do we want to make?

> The phone's persistent ringing shattered the silence. Alan ran down the hall, his heart racing. A 2 am call is never good news.
>
> 'I'm coming back to the city.' It was the alcohol-assisted voice of his best friend. 'I like the work well enough, but I can't live on this kind of money. There is no job in this village that will pay me what I need to live the lifestyle that I want.'
>
> 'Didn't you know that when you moved out there?' Alan was blunter than usual, but then the small hours of the morning would do that to him.
>
> 'I knew the numbers, but I didn't really know what they meant – if that makes sense.'
>
> Alan understood: his business had just made exactly the same mistake.

How much money you want to make is a key question – especially for small and medium-sized businesses and particularly for those just starting up.

Too many small businesses start with a model that will not generate enough money for their owners and will never give them enough to buy what they need to create a good future.

It is a simple but powerful question to keep in mind throughout the strategic planning process. Spend a few minutes right now sketching out the costs of doing business (and add 20 per cent) and the amount you need above those costs.

Consider the risks you are taking and add up what your lifestyle requires – now and in the future. Make sure that this figure is going to be comfortably achievable even in a poor year. If it isn't – do something else, reconsider your approach or accept this is a 'lifestyle choice', and start with the expectation that you will not be able to enjoy some of life's little luxuries.

Now, this might seem a little harsh. Even a breakeven florist has the opportunity to escape from basic income levels to enjoy financial success, if the model is to have a number of stores, or to franchise, or to deliver services at low cost, or just to have a really good location. However, you should know all this before you start. You should know that the first store is the first step, not the end point for the dream. Forecasting out the money and knowing your figure for how much you want to make is an important part of the strategic process.

For those of you in a big organization that is shovelling away impressive amounts, this is less of a critical question (most of this is dictated by a CEO, a Board or by market pressure). However, you may find it interesting to ask this question about yourself. How much do you need to earn to enjoy your chosen lifestyle and be able to fund your retirement? If you are falling short, then the remedy is obvious. If you are well in excess of the required figure, then you may want to pause and reflect on what you are doing and why. (Not really part of strategic planning I know... but worth a thought.)

What do we have to do to sustain optimal levels of performance?

Once you have asked the questions 'How do we create value for our customers and for ourselves?' and 'What are the areas of greatest opportunity?' and implemented a change plan, you will have got close to becoming optimized. The chances are that you will not stay in that state for long. Sub-optimization is strangling just about every organization in the world.

As soon as you install a brilliant process, the people at the front line will introduce minor variations, the supervisors will make amendments, and special circumstances will drive distortions. After a while that brilliant process has too many steps and it costs too much. Assume that any part of your business that is optimized today may take only two or three years to degrade by 10 to 20 per cent, and then continue to go downhill.

Sustaining optimum performance is particularly difficult, because we are accustomed to looking at businesses to determine if they are efficient or effective. Most management theories are built on these two foundations, and therefore most ways to diagnose business performance are based on these two organizing principles. On their own they are not enough. Optimization questions are different in nature. In the next chapter you will be applying a sub-optimization analysis. For the moment, think about sub-optimization in your business under the following headings: the persistent use of optimization questions, and the sustenance of myths.

The persistent use of optimization questions

The CEO listened patiently as the division heads paraded their most striking graphs and told their most boastful stories. The business was booming – there was no doubt about it.

However, the CEO had been around for long enough to see this before. She had felt the sting of a recession and watched it turn all those graphs upside down. She was deliberate with her questions:

- Are we the best at what we do, and how we do it?

- How do we know that for a fact?

- Where are the gaps?

- What are we doing to close those gaps?

She didn't want to deflate a buoyant team, but she did want to keep their attention on where there was lost opportunity. She knew that if the business could stay optimized, then it would be unassailable; if not – then its closest competitor would eat it up.

Consider your organization. How many questions are asked that look for what is missing? Listen out for these the next time you are in a meeting. You probably won't hear that many – maybe none at all. We are simply not used to challenging ourselves in this way, and we can easily start to lose ground inch by inch until we are so far behind that catching up is a significant effort. Strangely, but at the same time unsurprisingly, it is when we are at our most successful, when the money is rolling in and there seems to be no shortage of customers and opportunities, that we are most likely to channel all our resources into delivery. In our success it is easy to believe that it will always be this good and to under-invest in making improvements for the future.

The sustenance of myths

> 'I can tell which stores a Regional Manager visits, just by reading the figures. That's the power of the Regional Managers – they are worth their weight in gold.'

This was a myth that had persisted for years. Everyone believed that it was true. However, a careful look at the figures proved that store performance was influenced by a whole range of variables, such as the weather, day of the week, who was having a sale, and so on. The presence or absence of a Regional Manager made no difference whatsoever.

> 'Here are our top 20 customers. These are the ones that we need to look after. The business depends on them.'

A closer look showed that these customers were the largest 20 by volume of business, but with the discounts, time lavished on the accounts and special deals, every one – every single one – was costing more than they paid.

These are two of many myths that I have come across. Most businesses have several. They form the foundations for decisions that sap the strength of the business, and they make people focus in the wrong places.

Think about your business. List some of the facts that are taken as true. Start to ask for hard evidence that supports these facts. Be prepared to be surprised.

So, you are now ready to approach the task of gathering data with a set of questions and models in mind and with a strategic perspective into which you can insert your findings. Let's move on to Chapter 2 and find out what you need to understand about the engine of your strategic success – your customers.

Watch the video 'How to Think like a Strategist' at **www.koganpage.com/ editions/the-strategic-planning-workbook/9780749465001** to see Neville outlining the key messages in this chapter.

What are they thinking?
Customer analysis

There they are. A motley crowd. The elderly lady who smells of mothballs, the girl with flame red hair and an outbreak of facial piercing, the perspiring businessman who keeps on looking at his watch, the lady with dark circles around her eyes pushing a pram, the middle-aged man in overalls talking too loudly on his mobile phone. They are your customers. Bless them. But, analysing this lot – where do you start?

Ask people in an organization to describe their customers and they will tell you about 'difficult customers', 'big customers', 'important customers' and so on. They will say things about customers that those who are squeamish will not be able to write down. They will tell you about the customers who buy a lot of the product or service (and often use a considerable amount of resources) and those who get favourable attention for other reasons. These are all interesting ways to think about customers, but they are not particularly useful for making decisions.

To analyse customers you need to make two key distinctions. The first is between existing customers (covered in this analysis) and potential customers (see the next analysis). Once these distinctions are clear, you need to examine existing customers in two ways – from your point of view and from the customer's point of view.

The customer from your point of view

The customer is the source of the money that keeps your organization going. There are many ways to analyse customers, but the most powerful is to ask two key questions: 1) how much money do we make (total per year) and, 2) is this customer going to provide us with continuing business in the future? There are two ways that you should present this information: rank order for all customers and rank order by segment.

Just before we start to do this analysis – the first of several we are going to do together in this chapter – it is worth pointing out that this one is the most complex. That does not mean that it is difficult, but it will probably take you the longest to complete. I am telling you this now, so that you do not flip forward through the book and start to fret that all the others are going to be the same. Also, this is the most detailed analysis that you are going to complete. The reason is that customers are your greatest asset. You may have seen posters that say that your employees or your shareholders are your greatest assets – these are wrong. It all starts and ends with customers.

Rank order – total customers

This analysis is not really for a business like a department store where you have many thousands of customers, and even the largest one is a small fraction of your business. If you are in this kind of situation then you might like to identify your top 100 customers for interest (and some information which might be useful), but you are going to find your time better spent looking at your customer data by segment.

For everyone else this is going to be very interesting. To complete the analysis of the customers from your point of view, the first step is to develop a list of all your customers which shows the absolute amounts (in currency) that you gain from each customer: that is, the total sales in pounds (or dollars, or Euros) per year. Rank order this list so that the customer that buys the greatest amount of your product/service is at the top of the list, the one that buys the second largest amount is second, and so on. Use your figures for the past 12 months to complete this calculation if they are available, or use annual sales figures. This kind of information should be available in your accounting, sales and billing records.

Have a look at this list. You will probably have a set of reasonably familiar customers towards the top of this list, and then a large number of customers who have only spent a tiny amount with you in the past 12 months at the bottom. You should decide if it is worth completing any further analysis on this 'tail'. Typically the top 30 to 40 per cent will be the customers with whom you want to have/will have an ongoing relationship, and typically the rest will be 'once off' or 'nuisance customers' who will collectively represent less than 10 per cent of your income. It is entirely legitimate to narrow your focus at this stage (but if you decide to chop off the tail do not throw this list away – we will look at it again when we analyse costs). However, use a bit of judgement: if you think that many of these customers that represent a lesser value to you may become important to you in the future, then keep some or all of them.

Now, analyse the amount of growth likely in the next 12 months for each customer on your list. This information will probably be part of sales forecasts, but if it is not written down, ask the sales people concerned for their realistic (which means conservative for most people in sales) expectations.

Express this growth as a percentage, so if you are doing $100,000 worth of business today and you expect to be doing $140,000 in the next 12 months, this is a 40 per cent increase, and you write this as +40 per cent. If you were doing $100,000 and you expect that this will fall to $60,000 in the next 12 months then this would be –40 per cent.

Next, complete a similar exercise, but instead of looking ahead 12 months, analyse/guesstimate where you will be in three years' time in relation to today's level of business. So, if you were doing $100,000 worth of business at the moment, $140,000 in 12 months and $160,000 in three years, you would put +60 per cent. Do not factor in any changes that you think may come out of this strategic planning process – assume that you will continue much the same as you are today.

Put this information into a four-column table, as in Table 2.1. Calculate the total value for the past 12 months, the next 12 months, and the next three years and put these in the total row.

Now draw a line in yellow highlighter at the point where 80 per cent of the value for that column is achieved (all the amounts above that line add up to 80 per cent of the total). Also, draw a line in blue highlighter at the point that represents 20 per cent of the customers on your list. These lines will probably be at different places in each column.

This is an interesting analysis. Let us do another one that is more interesting again. Go back to your list of customers and this time work out the profit per customer (not just the total amount of money that you gain from

TABLE 2.1   Customer value by total sales

Customer name	Total value $ (for the past 12 months)	Likely growth over the next 12 months	Likely growth over the next 3 years
	Total:	Total:	Total:

TABLE 2.2   Customer value by profit

Customer name	Total value $ (for the past 12 months)	Likely growth over the next 12 months	Likely growth over the next 3 years
	Total:	Total:	Total:

them). To calculate the profit you need to look at the amount you gain (you have that) and the costs incurred. Do not try and make this too complicated by looking at costs of funds or lost opportunity – or you will retire before you complete this exercise. Rather, look at the time invested (you will probably have timesheets or some kind of job code) and the cost of the materials and distribution (and any other obvious and recognizable costs in your business) and the gross margin (if you have this). If none of this information is readily available, ask the people in your business who are most likely to know to estimate the effort and materials involved. If you have to do this, then put a confidence level on this figure (if you are only 80 per cent confident that the data are right, then express the number as a range, that is +/–20 per cent of the number you calculated, so a guesstimate of $100,000 that is probably only 80 per cent correct is expressed as a range of $90,000–$110,000).

Now put this information into a four-column table like the one in Table 2.2. Once again put a yellow highlight line in each column to show when 80 per cent of the value has been achieved, and draw a blue line below the top 20 per cent of customers.

You have now completed the most challenging analysis in this book, and you are now looking at a comprehensive picture of where your money is coming from today, and where it is likely to come from in the future. You could even perform a calculation, based on the numbers and forecasts, which will show how much money you will make in the next three years (this is an indication only – do not get depressed or excited yet).

Rank order by segment

Earlier in this book we considered the question 'What business are we in now?' You completed a brief exercise that outlined the customer segments served by your organization. Now we need to get a little more scientific.

Identifying your segments makes it easier to target your products/ services. The better you target, the more successfully you will meet the needs of your customers, and the more likely it is that you will achieve both high margins and happy customers. There are many different ways to segment your customers. The best segmentation approaches are those that have the following characteristics:

- actionable – you can do something different to appeal to the different segments;
- sustainable – the segments are enduring over time, not just in the short term;
- simple – the segments are not too difficult to define, so you can readily identify the characteristics of a particular segment;
- explanatory – they explain something about customer behaviour.

These questions help you to identify your segments:

- Can you identify the types of people in each segment using key demographics (age, gender, income, etc)?
- Does it make more sense to segment by geographies (where they live, where they work, etc)?
- Do your customers naturally fall into different categories by the types of organizations they work for, or the size of the organization that they come from?
- Are there clear user types based on how they apply or gain benefits from your products/services?
- Is price sensitivity a key way to categorize your customers?
- How might you communicate differently to these different segments?
- Will you modify your offer to appeal to these different groups? If so, how?

The chances are that one or two will be the obvious choices for your business, and you can then develop your strategy with these segments in mind. If no easy segments 'jump out' at you, then I suggest that you segment your organization by analysing the different types of customers who buy the different types of products/services.

Here is an easy way to complete this analysis. You will need the help of the front line in your organization, so you will need to convene a couple of focus groups. You will also need a whole stack of different magazines (leisure, business, general interest, women's and so on – just ask people to bring in old copies of the stuff they like to read), and several large cardboard sheets.

Ask the people in the focus group to consider a specific product/service. Ask them to describe the kinds of customers who typically buy that product/service. Now ask them to cut out pictures that most closely represent the different types of customers (what they are like, what they do for work and leisure, what sort of house they live in, where they go on holidays, etc) and to stick the different images on to the cardboard sheets. When they have completed their set of collages, ask them to provide a bullet point list of reasons that these customers buy, the benefits they receive, and an estimated percentage of the volume of business that each customer group represents – in sales revenue per year. All the percentages together should total 100 per cent. These bullet point lists and revenue estimates need to be verified by further research, but they are worth collecting at this time.

Keep doing the focus groups for the different products that you provide. The chances are that after a few you will find that the same customer groups are identified. When you have a full set, develop names for each segment.

Now that you have identified your segments, create a four-column table, like the one in Table 2.3. This time, list the segments and allocate your customers to the right segment. So you will see a heading for the segment, and a list of the customers that belong to that segment in the first column. You already have the information for each customer, so simply enter this in the remaining columns. Add up the values for each segment, now and into the future.

Complete a similar exercise, but this time for profit by segment, using the data that you already have. Enter the information in Table 2.4.

TABLE 2.3   Segment by value

Segment	Total value $ (for the past 12 months)	Likely growth over the next 12 months	Likely growth over the next 3 years
Segment A			
	Total:	Total:	Total:
Segment B			
	Total:	Total:	Total:
Segment C			
	Total:	Total:	Total:

TABLE 2.4 Segment by profit

Segment	Total value $ (for the past 12 months)	Likely growth over the next 12 months	Likely growth over the next 3 years
Segment A			
	Total:	Total:	Total:
Segment B			
	Total:	Total:	Total:
Segment C			
	Total:	Total:	Total:

You now have an idea of where your organization is centred, and which segments will lead the way in the future.

This is a powerful exercise. You now have four straightforward tables that lay bare the value delivered to your organization by your customers today, and the likely future value of the different customers and segments. Typically this kind of analysis shows you that some of the customers you have always treasured as 'the best' are costing you almost as much as they deliver, and it may well emerge that the customers you have paid little attention to are those upon whom the future of your organization depends.

Sources of information

In all likelihood the information you need is already stored in some way. At the very least there will be a record of the invoices sent to customers. The first place to look is in the finance department. Ask them to gather information about the money. The second place to look is in the sales areas. They should have data about sales per customer and discounts given, along with forecasts and projections. If they do not have the data you need, they will probably want to help you find it – it is somewhat useful for day-to-day decision making. The next place to gather information is the time recording systems (and customer codes). Hopefully these will tell you how much time is expended with each customer so you can add this information to the costs of the product information and margin data to work out the return on sales.

Customers – from their point of view

> The hotel just didn't deliver what it promised. Of course the lobby was very elegant and the food was excellent (if eye-wateringly expensive), but the room was a disappointment. The hot water fluctuated from icy to scalding, the fridge noisily turned on and off all night, waves of hotel staff barged in during the day to check or refresh things and there was that faint odour of something not all together pleasant. Sarah made a mental note never to stay there again.

Customers see your business from a completely different perspective. They have only peripheral interest in how much they are contributing to your bottom line. Some care about your capacity to generate enough to stay in business (because it would create a small amount of annoying decision making if you were to go broke), others have no interest at all. (Of course, if you are a bank your customers are keenly interested in your well-being because you are holding their money – but few businesses are in this category).

The better you understand customers from their point of view, the more likely it is that you will secure more of the business you want at the margin that you hope for. The more closely your strategy is aligned to meeting both your needs and those of your customers, the more likely it is that you will share a bright future.

Here is a list of the key information that you need:

- What criteria your customers use to judge your products/services.
- Why the customer buys your product/service.
- Why the customer prefers your product/service to those of your competitors.
- How satisfied your customers are with your product/service.
- Who makes the decision to buy and continue to buy your products/ services – and what criteria they use.

This set of data shows you where you have weaknesses that will affect future profits, it foreshadows customer problems, and it illustrates the strengths that you can emphasize. I will overview what each piece of information tells you, and then describe how you can collect this set of data in the next section, 'How to understand your customers from their point of view'.

What criteria your customers use to judge your products/services (hallmarks of success analysis)

The criteria that we use to assess our world drive our decisions. The more successfully you can make these criteria explicit, the more you can deliberately use them to shape outcomes.

The 'hallmarks of success' analysis forces people to identify what is really important and what truly underpins success. It is one of my favourite techniques because it is really straightforward, and really powerful. It can be applied to all kinds of different questions, and it almost always reveals something that people did not fully understand.

The 'hallmarks of success' analysis helps you to identify the distinguishing features that make organizations of your kind successful in your industry. It then shows you how close you come to possessing those features, and what you need to do to improve.

Here is how it works. Create a four-column table like the one in Table 2.5. Pick between five and ten people in your organization who have the best and clearest insights about the industry you are in, and who are not immune to recognizing faults in your own business.

First, ask them to think about those organizations in your industry that are successful and unsuccessful. Ask them to picture one that is the most successful, and one that is the least successful. Now ask them this question: 'What are the four to six key features that make the difference between the successful and the unsuccessful organization, and which therefore deliver success to the best performing organizations?' Record their answers, and then ask them to rank order that list. Show the rank order in the next column.

Now ask them to score each item on that list to show the extent to which your organization possesses that feature. A score of 1 means that you have this more than any other organization, 3 means that you are about average and 5 means that this feature is not strongly in evidence. You can use the

TABLE 2.5 Hallmarks of success analysis

Feature	Rank	Current performance	Improvement opportunity

scores 4 and 2 to provide some shading. In the fourth column record their suggestions about what needs to be improved. You should ask for ideas, even when there is a score of 1.

Once five to ten people have offered their insights you can put their answers together. The chances are that there will be several features that everyone nominated (look at the meaning, not just the words) and only a couple that are unique to just one person. Rank order this list by the number of times that a feature was selected, so you will have the ones that everyone suggested at the top of the list. Now combine the scores that people gave and produce an average. This table will show you what you need to do to be successful.

Now complete the same analysis, but this time with five to ten customers. The same basic process applies. Find a sample of customers – or if you want more specific and relevant information, a sample of customers in a particular segment who enjoy the benefit of a defined set of products/services. Ask them to think about all the organizations that provide them with the kinds of products and services they currently buy from you. Ask them to identify the features that separate those that get it right from and those that do not. As before, ask them to score where you rate compared with the others, and ask them to suggest improvement opportunities. Enter their responses on a similar table. Now highlight the similarities and differences between what your own people identified and what the customers believed was important.

This is a really great technique. You can probably imagine all kinds of other situations where you can use it to surface information that will underpin decisions. Essentially it makes you escape from your own way of viewing the world, and forces you to see the world from the point of view of the recipient of the outcomes that you provide. You could even try it on your life partner (but don't call me if you spend the night talking about relationship renewal).

Why the customer buys your product/service

> 'When it leaves the factory it is lipstick – when it is opened by the customer it is hope.'

It is particularly important to understand the value that your customer extracts from your product/service. You might sell a tangible product, say a car, but the benefits derived by your customers may be entirely separate from the transportation capabilities of the vehicle. Customers may buy it because they feel 'cool'. It is important to understand your customers' needs.

Needs

Needs are the fundamental expectations. There are two kinds: rational needs and emotional needs.

Rational needs are the objective requirements. The product or service has to meet these to fulfil its purpose. So, a protective garment has to keep you warm, survive the washing process and still be waterproof.

Emotional needs are at a deeper level, and are about what wearing a specific brand says about you, and how you feel in it and about it. People pay many times more for a garment with the same functionality as its cheaper cousin because it has a brand value.

With this distinction in mind, consider your own favourite fashion statement. Consider the pleasure you got from a special pair of shoes, a leather jacket, an outrageously expensive handbag, an up-market watch, an item of jewellery, a tattoo, or whatever you bought with a psychological pay-off. There is little that can be categorized as rational in any of these purchases, but the feel-good value is huge.

This is not easy information to extract and understand, because sometimes customers only have a shallow understanding about the motivating factors that drive their decision-making processes. Careful interviewing and well-constructed focus group questions (along with some introspection as to what you really like about your products and services) will yield some powerful data.

On the list of likely psychological/emotional needs will be:

Attention	Appreciation
Dignity	Respect
Independence	Freedom
Anxiety resolution	Protection
Nurturing	Love
A sense of mastery	Self-respect
Leadership	Stability
Inner harmony	Control
Feeling sexy	Feeling cool
A sense of camaraderie	

So, while the people in your organization may be particularly proud of the technical brilliance of the product, customers may be totally uninterested in the problems that have been conquered. They just want the solution delivered by your product/service and the psychological value it delivers. The better you can understand customers' true motivations, the easier it is to centre your product/service on what will make them buy, and the more likely it is that they will come back.

Why the customer prefers your product/service to those of your competitors

Customers have the choice to buy from someone else. They make the choice to stay with you every week, maybe every day. Every time they see a competitor's advertisement, every time they read a magazine that mentions a benefit they are not receiving, every time they receive an item of direct mail from someone else that makes an attractive offer – they make that choice. So why do they stay with your organization?

The more closely you understand this, the easier it is to concentrate your effort on those aspects that are unique to your business and that customers truly value, then the more deliberately you can drive a wedge between your organization and your nearest competitors. Using the techniques described later in this chapter (particularly focus groups) you should ask what customers like and dislike about your products and services, what they like and dislike about your competitors' offerings and what would be their 'switching point'.

How satisfied your customers are with your product/service

> Profits jumped again. When he took over the store it was already performing well, but every month the figures just got better and better. Now James was a real hero in the business. The CEO had said so.
>
> After six months the profits stabilized. The next month they started to fall. In the following three months they plummeted to a record low, and stayed in free-fall for the following 12 months.

The problem for James was customer satisfaction. He had achieved those impressive profits by cutting back on staff, casual hours, maintenance and cleaning. The once-friendly store was sparsely served by overworked staff, and the place just did not look and feel the same. Experienced employees resigned and loyal customers stopped coming back. Once the staff and customers were gone... they were gone. For good. There was no getting them back. It took that store several years to return to the pre-James days.

Customer satisfaction is a key performance measure in many organizations. There is a good reason for this. Dissatisfied customers look around for alternative suppliers of the product/service, they typically make more demands and force greater discounts or concessions while they are in the process of searching, and they use more of your resources. At the same time they tell their colleagues and friends not to do business with you.

Satisfied customers will be more profitable, will be more likely to buy a fuller range of your products/services (and more of then) and generate opportunities for you to meet new potential customers. Falling or low levels of customer satisfaction show that you need a remedial programme now, and they foreshadow a downturn in the level of activity, or profit – or both – with that customer. For the purposes of the strategic plan you need to identify three levels of satisfaction: 'not satisfied', 'satisfied' and 'more than satisfied'.

Who makes the decision to buy and continue to buy your products/services – and what criteria they use

Customers may gain a number of different benefits at different levels, and you may have some strong supporters of your organization within your customer base, but all this counts for little if the decision to continue to buy your products/services rests with one person. If this is the case, you need to be particularly knowledgeable about how this person views your organization and what he or she values. There is no magical technique to use to collect this information – you have to talk to him or her. For this strategic process you need to develop a three-column table, like the one in Table 2.6, list of the key buyers, and then show how critical that particular individual is to your business (on a scale of 1–10) and the strength of your relationship with them (on a scale of 1–10).

TABLE 2.6   Buyer analysis

Buyer	Criticality of this person	Strength of relationship

So, we know what to look for; let's learn some research techniques in the next chapter.

03 Getting into their heads
How to understand your customers

The only way to get reliable data about customers is to ask them. An organization only knows 30 per cent of what is going on in its customers' heads, the rest comes from research.

You have already completed some solid thinking. Create a five-column table like Table 3.1 and fill in the first two columns to summarize what you have achieved so far:

TABLE 3.1 Key customer data

Product	Segment/customers for this product	Why the customers buy	Advantages from the customers' point of view	Level of satisfaction

You now need to gather accurate information to complete this table. If you are lucky you will have conducted a customer survey in the recent past, and it should contain most of this information. If the report is presented as pages of statistics, ask those who completed the research to summarize their notes and working papers. It is here that you will find interviews with the key people and other data that will give richness and texture to pages of numbers.

If you are not so fortunate, there are four techniques that will give you all the information you need. They are listed from the least to most expensive, and are: observation, talking, focus groups and surveys.

Observation

This is straightforward, powerful, and yields a remarkable amount of information. It simply involves observing customer behaviour. This type of research can be conducted by almost anyone in the organization, from a junior employee through to senior management.

Observation research also gives senior managers the chance to learn about the many subtle activities that make up the service interactions, and the interplay of these elements. A report about the number of complaints does not live in the memory in the same way as a red-faced customer who clearly feels that he or she has been ill-treated by your organization. The chance to see what aspects of their experience give customers the most pleasure creates an image that is far more compelling than a graph.

Think about your business. Where do queues form, where do the large volumes of calls arrive, where do customers form initial impressions? Go to one or several of those places and find a spot where you can be reasonably unobtrusive, then quietly observe what is going on. Look at the faces of customers to see when they register surprise, frustration, pleasure and so on. Note if there are common experiences that seem to drive those reactions. Now, look at your frontline employees. Note what they find difficult and easy, what they do to provide service, how long it takes, and what reactions they produce.

A few hours of observation will provide you with amazingly rich information. If you have not observed your customer contact people for a while, you will be in for a surprise of some kind – guaranteed.

Talking

This is so simple it is often overlooked or underrated by organizations. So who should you be talking to? There are two groups: customers and employees.

Customers

You can learn so much by asking good questions and then being quiet and listening to the answers. Such discussions need not be formalized research projects – a maître d', for instance, can learn a lot about his or her customers simply by moving around the restaurant tables. A mechanic can understand his or her customers better by investing more time at either end of the service process. A shopkeeper can ask questions to discover what customers really value.

Next time you are with a customer, try asking one, or all, of these questions:

- How do you use our products/services (ask him or her to describe what he or she does, step by step)?
- What do you particularly like about our products/services?
- Tell me one thing we could do differently next time.
- What was the best part of your experience with us today?
- What changes would you make, if this were your business?

Be careful to listen objectively. Some golden rules for listening are:

- Avoid becoming defensive. Listen to the description of the problem rather than trying to find an excuse.
- Avoid attributing blame. Listen to what is being said rather than trying to picture who you are going to yell at later on.
- Provide encouragement to the customer to share information honestly and openly.
- Encourage the customer to express emotions as well as relate facts.
- Thank the customer for his or her useful feedback.

This will help you to understand how your customers feel about your organization.

Employees

Front-line employees have an extraordinary understanding about what customers buy, how they use the product/service and how satisfied they are. The problem is that they do not organize what they know in a way that makes it accessible to anyone else. Sometimes the people in front-line positions do not know what they know – until you tease it out of them with some good questions.

There are two straightforward ways to gain good front-line data. The first is to talk to them individually. Simply take a tour around the front-line positions and ask questions like:

- What is your greatest frustration at the moment?
- What seems to be the greatest frustration the customers are having at the moment? What do you think we could do to fix these frustrations?
- What do the customers seem to like the most?
- What one change could we make that would make what we do more attractive to the customers?

Be careful not to be defensive when you ask these questions. (If you are, people will quickly work out that you do not really want the truth, and they will not give it to you.) Also, make sure that you let people know when you have made changes based on what they have told you.

The second way is to have front-line focus groups. These can be relatively informal groups of five to eight people, perhaps over a sandwich lunch. You can ask much the same questions that you asked individuals, but this time you can see people's reactions to what others say, and you help the group to build on ideas.

A considerable amount of information about your organization – and your customers – resides in the heads of the front-line people, information that is never captured in any formal system. If you can unlock just a fraction of this you will be in a position to provide considerably better service, probably at a significantly reduced cost.

Focus groups

Focus groups are relatively easy to design and conduct. There are seven steps that you need to complete to run a focus group successfully:

1 Invite groups of people that you are interested in (ie current customers, lapsed customers, etc). Make sure they are representative of that group and sufficiently articulate to generate useful discussion.

2 Ensure each group is relatively homogeneous in terms of demographic characteristics (ie a similar age group, or split up males and females if their views are likely to be different).

3 Make sure the moderator (person running the session) is objective. He or she should not provide feedback in any way, but simply facilitate relevant discussion.

4 Develop a clear purpose for the session. You might want to find out what customers like/do not like, what they expect you to do in different situations, how you compare to others, and so on. Make sure you have a set of questions that ensure you achieve that purpose.

5 Avoid a 'gripe' session by carefully facilitating insightful discussion at both a rational and emotional level. This might involve getting the group members to develop options (rather than focusing on their problems).

6 Reward customers for attending. This does not need to be a cash reward (although external research agencies do pay people). It might be a voucher or free service offer. The main purpose of the reward is to thank them for their time and reimburse personal expenses incurred in coming to the group. However, it is not the money that makes a difference – most customers simply need to know that their opinions and ideas have truly been valuable to your organization.

7 Ensure that feedback from the group is summarized into a set of action plans.

Once you have conducted this focus group you will know what the people in the room think and feel. If you run several focus groups and get much the same responses, then you can form an opinion that all customers think and feel the same way. For most strategic planning exercises you have probably collected enough information. You are not trying to design a full service strategy at this stage. However, if you want more, then you need to do a survey.

Surveys

Quantitative research measures the elements that were uncovered in the focus groups through surveys or questionnaires. While it is relatively simple to design and conduct a survey, it is time-consuming and there are a number of traps that need to be avoided. You need to be sure that you have followed the golden rules:

- Make sure that every question explores only one variable. So, for example, do not ask a question like, 'How would you rate the friendliness and efficiency of our staff?' You might get a poor score and not know whether it is because your staff are friendly but inefficient, or efficient but unfriendly, or both unfriendly and inefficient. Instead, ask both elements as separate questions.

- Design questions so that you know how to interpret the score. Ask yourself 'What would I do with a high/low score on this question?' If there is no obvious action, then you need to redesign so that the answer to every question compels you to do something.

- Do not have extreme questions of the kind 'I am always extremely satisfied with...'. No one will agree with this (no organization is that great), and it will distort the findings.

- Make the questions as simple as possible – remember the average reading age in the UK is around the level of an 8-year-old.

- Use as many 'closed' questions as possible. These are questions that force customers to respond using a point on a scale rather than write in whatever they like as an answer. Closed questions are much easier to analyse.

- Do not have too many questions. People quickly get bored. The longer it takes to complete the questionnaire, the more chance you have of getting 'made up' responses towards the end of it. Aim for a questionnaire that can be completed in less than 10 minutes to get the best response.

- Test the questions before you use them to make sure that what you think they mean is interpreted in the same way by customers.

- Ask the right questions of the right customers. You need to identity which characteristics within your segments you need to explore.

- Analyse the data so that the key points shine through. You will produce a telephone book of paper as part of the analysis. Do not present this. Instead, develop graphics that show the greatest gaps and priorities.

- Develop a report that describes the survey in plain English, with lots of charts and pictures and as few numbers as possible. This report need not be a written document, and should be in a form that will have the most impact on your organization (see Chapter 7).

- Prepare the senior managers in your organization for the results. This means involving them right from the beginning and making them aware of the implications of high and low scores. Ask them to guess at the results before they arrive – it sharpens their interest when they find out if their guesses were correct.

- Prepare a straightforward summary of the results that you can give to the front line. This should include the findings of the survey and the actions that your organization will take as a result. The better front-line staff understand your customers and how you want them to respond, the better they will be at delivering the right customer experience.

You can conduct this survey in a number of different ways. You can:

- send it in the post (but be sure to send a reply-paid envelope);
- give it to customers and ask them to complete it on the spot;
- conduct it over the phone;
- send it electronically (by e-mail or post it on a website).

Essentially, the less contact you have with recipients, the less likely it is that they will complete the questionnaire. By post you may get a 1–5 per cent return (depending on who you are and the issue). On the phone you may get a 10–20 per cent response rate, but the phone is considerably more expensive. You might get good responses with a questionnaire posted on the internet, but remember that your sample might end up being skewed to technology-proficient customers.

Sources of information

These include any form of customer survey, any customer satisfaction measures, any reports that show performance service against service standards. Also, look at your competitors' websites or any other public information. They may have conducted customer surveys and they may report those findings along with some details.

So, you now have some good ways to understand your customers, and by using your preferred technique (or a combination) you can complete the table you began at the start of this chapter. You have nearly completed your customer research, but there is still one group to go – potential customers.

Who else is out there?
Potential customer analysis

Out there in 'customer land' are the potential customers who will deliver your future success. You just need to find them.

Potential customers can come from three key sources:

1 Customers for the products/services you provide who are buying from your competitors.

2 Customers who are not yet buying the products/services you (and others) provide.

3 Customers you could have, if you developed your business in a different direction.

Customers for the products/services you provide who are buying from your competitors

First make a list of the customers you know are buying from your competitors, who have a natural fit with the kinds of customers that you have today. They might be in the same industry, be about the same size, or have the same kinds of needs. Now make a five-column table and put this list in the first column; see Table 4.1.

In the second column write down your best estimate of the worth of those customers, in sales revenue per year. You might know this because your customer tells you, your competitors may have made this public in

TABLE 4.1   Potential customers who are buying from the competition

Potential customers	Value of these customers (revenue $ per year)	Competitors' attraction	Our response	Likelihood of success

some way (they may say how many units of product they sold in their annual report, or they might present some volumes at a conference), your sales people may know the customer's needs and how much of those needs are serviced by competitors, or you may know the industry well enough to have a good guess.

In the third column note the reason the customer buys from your competitor. If you are sure this reason is right, mark it down in black. If you are only guessing, use red.

In the fourth column note down what you think you would need to do to bring that customer's business into your organization. Again, use the red and black colour coding to show your level of confidence.

In the fifth column express the likelihood that you could attract the customer, as a percentage. So if you were 50 per cent confident that you would gain this customer's business, record 50 per cent; if you think that it is 80 per cent likely, record 80 per cent, and so on.

You can now perform a rough calculation to show the available money, and you can weight this by the percentage likelihood to show how much potential business is available to you if you could attract these customers.

Customers who are not yet buying the products/services you (and others) provide

These customers fall into two key groups: existing businesses that are yet to enter your marketplace, and new businesses that will start up in the near future.

TABLE 4.2   Potential customers who exist overseas

Potential customers	Value of these customers	Action required to secure this customer	Likelihood of success

Existing businesses

These may be organizations that already have a presence in another country or online, that have announced they will be beginning operations here. There may also be organizations that are diversifying and will require the kinds of products/services that you provide. You can keep track of these simply by reading the newspapers and magazines where they might advertise. Make a list of these potential customers, and then prepare a four-column table like the one in Table 4.2.

In the first column list these kinds of potential customers. In the second column estimate the potential value of the customer, in sales revenue per year. This is going to be a guesstimate, so use the most conservative numbers. In the third column note down what you think you might need to do to secure the available business. In the fourth column estimate the percentage likelihood that you will secure the business. Once again, you can perform an indicative calculation that shows the available money value, discounted by the likelihood that you will secure this customer.

New businesses that will start up in the near future

New businesses start up all the time. Some of these may need the kinds of products and services that you provide. You want to be the first to secure the right kinds of start-ups. This means analysing where those businesses are likely to be and how they are likely to announce their presence.

Make a list of the types of businesses that have placed orders with your organization in their start-up phases, or are likely to do so in the future. Make a list of the places where you will find these businesses (technology parks, shopping malls, city centres and so on). Calculate the value of these orders (over two years), and estimate the likely future (how much you are

TABLE 4.3   Potential customers who are yet to start their businesses

Potential start-up businesses	Likely locations	Value (in orders over two years)	Likely future of this business	Investment required

likely to sell them per year once established). Note the likely investment required to secure this business (time invested, reworking of your existing products/services, and so on). Place this information in a five-column table, like Table 4.3. Rank order this list so that the businesses requiring the least investment to achieve the greatest return appear at the top.

Customers you could have, if you developed your business in a different direction

This is a difficult kind of analysis to complete, and you may come back to this several times. You may even find yourself here again after you have run the first strategic workshop.

As mentioned earlier in this book, you already have existing contracts and obligations, you have already invested in equipment, technology and databases, you own intellectual property, you have developed expertise in your people in particular fields and you have customer relationships that predispose you to gaining particular orders. When you envision the customer direction that you could develop in, and the customers you could have, keep all these restrictions in mind. There is no point in dreaming about a future that is not (in some way) a continuation of where you are now.

With that in mind, create a list of the possible directions you could develop into. This list is remarkably easy to produce: it exists in your business right now – it is simply that no one has written it down yet.

Your senior people, and all those who are 'thinkers' in your business, have ideas about the different directions that your business could travel in. These ideas have evolved through discussions over lunch, ideas presented at conferences, competitor activity, articles in magazines, products offered by

TABLE 4.4   Expanded list of potential customers

Possible direction	Potential customers	Value over the first 24 months	Probable value in the future	Closeness of fit to the current business	Investment required	Likelihood of success

consultants, research grants requested by universities, and so on. Your managers are just waiting to have someone take their ideas seriously. All you have to do is ask them.

At this stage you run the risk of collecting far too much information in a format that is too tangled to analyse successfully. To avoid this problem create a seven-column table, like Table 4.4.

The first two columns are straightforward. List the possible directions in which your business could develop, then identify the customers that you would attract by pursuing that direction. The third column shows how much you would expect to gain (expressed as the value of the orders) for each customer over the first 24 months of following the possible direction. This figure is a guesstimate, but is grounded in reality if you collect some information about how much the potential customers are spending now, and you estimate how much of that you could gain if you were to offer a product/service. The next column – probable value in the future – shows how much you believe each customer will settle down to order each year.

The closeness of fit is an estimate of how well prepared you are as a business to perform in this new direction and for each customer. You need to consider if you have products/services that are similar and need only to be modified, or if you have to develop new products/services from scratch. Investigate if you already have some form of relationship with these potential customers, or if you have to work hard to establish a presence. Assess whether you have the skills in-house to service these customers, or if you need to hire new talent.

When you have considered these all together (along with anything else that you think may be important in your situation, such as intellectual property or distribution channels) then create a percentage figure that expresses your assessment of how close your business is to where it needs to be. One hundred per cent means that you have all you need in place. Any figure below means that something is missing. Zero per cent means that nothing is in place. Do not try to be too scientific; the point is not to get a perfect score that can be justified in a court of law, but rather to generate some data so that you can compare one direction and/or customer with another.

The investment required (in the next column) is an analysis of how much you need to spend in the first two years. This should include time invested in sales as well as product/service development, equipment required, new people required and so on. This should be expressed as the total amount of money needed.

The final column – the likelihood of success – is another percentage estimate. Consider the strength of the competition and what it would take to win customers from them, the state of the market and/or customers' business and how prosperous they will be, and the capacity that your organization has to get enthusiastically behind this new direction. Once again, 100 per cent means that you are fully confident that you will be successful, and 0 per cent means that you haven't got a snowball's chance in hell.

Now, rank order this information so that the direction that offers the greatest return with the highest chance of success with the closest fit to your current business is at the top of the list.

Sources of information

There is a surprising amount of information in the public domain. To win new business, organizations will often reveal details about their current customers in annual reports, brochures, presentations, on their websites and in fact sheets. In-house newsletters often contain a big block of information, and are typically freely and publicly available in the organization's lobby.

It is also worth creating a way for everyone in your organization to record all the snippets of information they come across that relate to potential customers. This can be an inbox, or a physical box. If all employees are involved in the search for information, you will quickly build valuable databases to support your efforts to gain new customers.

You now have a good picture of your current and potential customers. It would be great to have all of them to yourself – but there are sharks in the water. Let's get an understanding about your competitors.

Go to **www.koganpage.com/editions/the-strategic-planning-workbook/9780749465001** and choose 'Understanding your Customers' for the video that accompanies Chapters 2, 3 and 4.

05

What are they doing?
Competitor analysis

Dawn. The African Savannah.

A steady breeze from the south-east. Perfect conditions to get close to the lone male lion. The King of the Jungle, 450 lbs of mean muscle that can achieve 75 kph in less than 10 seconds.

The two photographers inched towards the big beast, cameras ready. This could be a cover shot.

Suddenly the savannah grass moved in great waves that rolled across the plain. The wind had changed. The lion was on its feet in a fraction of a second. Its nostrils flared as it zeroed in on the photographers' scents. Its hunter's eyes locked on to them.

One of the photographers carefully placed his photographic equipment on the ground and then started to run.

'Don't be stupid,' called out his colleague. 'You can't outrun a lion.'

'I don't have to,' he called over his shoulder. 'I only have to outrun you.'

Every organization has a competitor of some kind. Public sector monopolies need to keep an eye on potential outsourcing offers for some/all of what they do, multinationals clash directly on every level of product and service, mid-sized businesses chase the same customers, and small businesses find that price and product performance are defined by the expectations set by their competitors.

Competitor relationships

The force of competition is not equally distributed. When considering competitors, identify the relationship that you have with them. There are three ways that your organization is likely to interact:

1 in a dance;

2 as a participant in a waiting room;

3 as a member of a trawling fleet.

The competitor dance

Some organizations have few competitors, all of which are well known to the potential customers. These organizations need to deliberately differentiate their products and services from the others, and where the choice available to the customers is public and obvious – such as airlines, soft drinks and banks – they need constantly to monitor and respond to their competitors.

These organizations are locked together in the competitor dance. As in a dance, if the competitor takes a number of steps in one direction then the others need to respond in some way, often by following the leader. Finding some form of uniqueness, a point of differentiation and ways to secure loyalty, consumes significant time and resources.

The competitor waiting room

In the 'waiting room' the competitors are known to each other, but are seen to be independent and are differentiated (often by size). They do not compete head on, typically serving different segments of the same customers. They are in a 'waiting room' ready to be called on by the customers. Each presents the merits of their goods or services to the customer, but here there is no particular need to change these in response to competitor changes.

The competitor trawl

The dance is the mental model to describe close relationships between competitors. The waiting room covers larger numbers of competitors with larger numbers of customer segments. The trawl describes many players in search of a large pool of opportunities. Think about a fishing fleet ploughing through the oceans to hunt down shoals of fish. Here the size and number of boats affect the long-term size of the stock, and the overall performance of the whole fleet affects market price. However, on a day-to-day basis the boats have little effect on each other.

This situation occurs in some industries where there are many competitors that are not really known to the customer, the customer's choice is driven by factors other than product features, and competitors do not need to keep in step with what the others are doing. The more plentiful the customers, and the more accepted the nature of the product/service, the more competitors there will be. If the barriers to competing are low there will be an army of competitors (examples include professional service firms and speciality stores).

So, different organizations have different relationships with their competitors. The more tightly bound together you are with your competitors, the more effort you need to invest in understanding what they are doing. The bigger the number of players, and the more loosely you are connected to your competitors, the less time you need to spend on competitor research.

Therefore, you are only likely to be spending significant time and effort on competitor research if you are in a competitor dance, or sitting in a small waiting room. This means that you are probably only going to be interested if there are a few significant competitors, which makes this an easier exercise because the smaller the number of competitors, the easier it is to find the information. You are likely to find that all the players in your market are discussed in trade magazines/on websites, they will be at all the industry conferences, and be out there with advertisements and statistics.

Competitor analysis

You should find the information needed to answer the following questions:

- Who are your competitors?
- What are their products/services?
- How much of the available market do they own?
- What gives them their leverage?
- What gives them a price advantage?
- What is their current financial position?
- What are they likely to do next?

You should also consider your potential competitors, and find information to answer the following:

- Who are the potential competitors?
- How likely is it they will enter this market?
- What will they do to entice your existing customers?
- How much of a threat does this pose?

For the first seven questions above, you need to create a seven-column table; see Table 5.1. Use this table to record your answers to the key questions.

TABLE 5.1 Competitor analysis

Competitors	Products/ services	Market share	Leverage/ attractiveness	Price advantage	Financial position	Likely future

Who are your competitors?

This question is best answered by considering the competitors you have for each segment. If there are many competitors, only list those that pose the greatest threat to you. This list forms the first line of information on the seven-column table. Include your own organization (in a different colour) on the list.

What are their products/services?

In the next column list the products/services offered by each competitor that are in direct competition with your organization for each segment. You will probably find that you are competing with the same organizations in a number of different segments. If so, highlight these organizations – they are in some ways similar to your organization and you should keep a particularly careful eye on them. You will also probably find that there are competitors who you only see in one or two segments, and who offer only a couple of products or services. In a different colour, highlight any large organizations that compete with you in this way. These could be organizations that are feeling their way into your market.

How much of the available market do they own?

If there are only a few large players in a market, it is relatively easy to work out the size of the market and who has which share – most of the information is public or can be readily inferred. If there are many players you will have less confidence when you perform the calculation, but it is nevertheless better to have imprecise but indicative information than none at all.

Place your analysis of what percentage of the market you have in the next column. Have a careful look at this information. It is just possible that you have some unique offerings, where you have 100 per cent of the market. This is particularly good news (so long as it is profitable). Now rearrange your list so that each segment is shown in rank order by market share, with the organization with the largest share at the top of the list.

What gives them their leverage?

There are two attributes from the customer's point of view – foundation and leverage. Foundation attributes are those that every organization has to have to stay in business. These foundation attributes get you into the game. They are not particularly exciting for the customer, because customers expect that they will be in place.

Leverage attributes are where the action is. Leverage attributes make one competitor different from another and they are used to entice customers. Typically, once a leverage attribute starts to achieve success, then all the competitors for that customer copy that attribute. Over time the leverage attributes become common to all, expected, and are downgraded in the customer's eyes to become foundation attributes. This is how more and more items become included as standard features in our products.

So, what leverage attributes do your competitors have that you are not offering? These are likely to be easy to find because they will be prominently described on their website and in their brochures. List these in the leverage/attractiveness column.

What gives them a price advantage?

A price advantage can fuel the capacity to develop a leverage attribute. Get together a group of your people who know a lot about your competitors and brainstorm what might give them a price advantage (an established business may own premises and so have lower loan repayment/rental than your business, it may own the source of raw materials, etc). If there is a difference between your cost structure and that of your competitors, you should list the key reasons and place them in the next column.

What is their current financial position?

In some cases this information will be publicly available. Expert analysis in the media, annual reports and so on will let you know if your competitors are cashed up and ready to make price a battleground, if they are likely to be cautious with new investments, or if they are likely to be looking to consolidate.

This information should be entered in the sixth column. The best way to do this is as a score out of 5. A score of 1 means they are in a strong position,

3 means that they are no better or worse than all the others in the same market, and 5 means that they are in trouble. The scores 2 and 4 provide some shades of grey in the scale.

What are they likely to do next?

Knowing what your competitors are likely to do next helps you to pre-empt their next move, or at least be a rapid follower. Often your competitors' next moves are not a secret – they are splashed all over their websites, they are talking about them at conferences, and they are producing brochures that describe their forthcoming products/services and directions in some detail. In the final column of the table record likely next moves in line with each product.

You now have a reasonable picture of where you stand in relation to your competitors. Find three coloured highlighters that you have not used so far. Highlight those competitors that represent your greatest threat today. Highlight those that represent your greatest threat in the future. Highlight those that are no serious threat at all. Keep a careful eye on the first two from now on.

Who are the potential competitors?

The information you have about potential competitors is likely to be sketchy, and the table that you have used for all the other competitor information does not lend itself to include potential competitors. For potential competitors you need just four columns for your table; see Table 5.2.

TABLE 5.2   Potential competitor analysis

Potential competitor	Likelihood of entering the market	Likely approach to entice your customers	The degree of threat

The best way to populate this table with data is to ask those people in your organization who have the best networks within your industry to provide the list. Then use the same approach as you did with competitors to verify your information – check their websites, look at their brochures and so on. Rate the likelihood that they will enter the market on a scale of 1 to 5, with 1 representing the most likely. Rate the degree of threat on a scale of A, B, C, with A representing high threat, B moderate and C little.

Now highlight those potential competitors that are likely to enter the market and that represent a high threat. Compare their ways of attracting your customers to your ways of retaining those same customers.

Sources of information

All organizations are caught in the same dilemma. How much information should they keep secret so that their competitors are unable to match or build on their ideas, and how much do they need to make available so that their customers and potential customers know what is on offer? In reality, it is usually the marketing and sales people who make this kind of information available, and since they are more concerned with their sales targets than they are about preserving secrets, you will probably find that there is a lot of information in the public domain.

You will also find that people at conferences will share a lot of details and ideas – particularly at question time, and if you keep up a reasonable network of people in your industry then you will hear a whisper of a significant change well in advance of that change occurring. Also, do not forget that you may well employ people who until recently worked for your competitor. This does not give you the right to grill them about every detail, but if they volunteer information you should not ignore it.

As mentioned when considering potential customers, you should develop a place where employees can record all the shreds of information that they learn about competitors. This can be an e-mail address or physical location, and if you provide a really simple questionnaire for people to fill in to offer their intelligence, you will find it easier to collect, manage and make sense of the data.

Go to **www.koganpage.com/editions/the-strategic-planning-workbook/ 9780749465001** and choose 'Competitor Analysis' for a video summary of the key points in this chapter.

06 **Pressure points**
Understanding the driving forces in your industry

Listen to politicians in virtually any democratic country and they will tell you about how high inflation, unemployment, interest rates (or whatever) were when the opposition was in power. They will then provide comparative current figures and parade their 'accomplishments'. They will claim that the difference is all down to their skill as economic and social managers. The way the story is told these politicians are in complete command of all the variables.

This is, of course, a somewhat generous use of the truth. Countries, industries and companies are buffeted by all kinds of forces that bend their plans out of shape and change the rules they have to apply to be successful. The better you understand these forces, the more accurately you can predict what is likely to happen, the more effectively you can create accurate scenarios of the future – the more likely you are to be the buffeter rather than the buffeted.

Before you can develop a strategic plan that will chart the course to a more successful future, you need to be sure about your starting point and you need to see what lies ahead. To do this you need to apply some diagnostic tools that reveal how your strategic context really functions at a fundamental level.

Many different tools are used by strategists. Some require a lot of information and need to be analysed by advanced statistical and modelling packages. However, in many cases you do not need this kind of detail to make the right decisions about your future.

We have already seen ways to understand customers, potential customers and competitors. In this chapter we will cover:

- environmental analysis;
- barriers to entry analysis; and
- availability analysis.

In the next chapter I cover some diagnostic tools that help you to understand your internal context. These are:

- stakeholder analysis;
- culture analysis;
- skills matrix/talent analysis;
- financial performance analysis;
- process performance (using the sub-optimization analysis);
- risk analysis;
- resources versus outcomes analysis;
- cause and effect analysis;
- relative scale analysis (benchmarking);
- absolute scale analysis (using a framework); and
- change readiness analysis.

These tools help you to gather clear information. The clearer the information, the easier it is to make decisions later on. Some decisions will virtually make themselves when you have all the data gathered in one place. However, bear in mind that these tools are designed to surface facts, but they do not – in their own right – result directly in actions. They provide the inputs necessary for the next stage of the strategic planning process.

There will inevitably be many 'I never realized that' kinds of moments that this data will produce. Keep a note of what was most surprising, and remind people about their first reactions when you run the workshops later in the process, but do not be tempted to make any decisions until you arrive at the next chapter (see Chapter 13 on tricks and traps).

I have given you a number of ways to collect and present data. The chances are that even though you do not analyse your business in this way on a regular basis, most of the raw data that you need is available in some kind of system or another. If there is no formal system, it is probable that someone is keeping an informal record of the kind of data that you need, or it is in someone's head. In most cases organizations know what they need to know. They simply do not put that information together in a way that allows meaningful analysis and compels strategic questioning.

You need to gather the information carefully because, as mentioned before, in many organizations there are myths about how value is created and which customers return the greatest amount. You need good facts to dispel these myths, because if you take them into the analysis phase, then any existing weaknesses will be amplified.

Environmental analysis

There are six different types of environmental constraints that can crush your capacity to sustain profit, and ultimately survive. Alternatively, any one of these could open the door to a level of success that otherwise would have been impossible. These are:

1 physical environment;
2 political/legal/tax environment;
3 economic environment;
4 technological environment;
5 demographic environment; and
6 social environment.

I will outline these first, and then describe how you should collect and present the required data.

Physical environment

Some businesses depend on changes in seasons to stimulate activity. So, the fashion business needs a change in the weather to help it to convince people to invest in new wardrobes, temperature increases are required to boost drink and ice-cream consumption, tourist numbers are affected by the blazing summer or the drenching wet season, and so on. The cycle of the seasons is important to a number of organizations. If you are one of these organizations this will already be a significant topic of conversation in your business.

Also, there is the physical environment we live in. The evidence shows that the world is warming, the climate is changing and the billions of tonnes of carbon dioxide we release into the atmosphere every year is the primary cause. As carbon pricing becomes global, as environmental lobbies become ever stronger, and as public awareness about climate change develops, organizations that have a carbon-related effect on the world need to factor in changes (of all kinds) in managing their environmental impacts.

Unless you have been living in a cave for the past couple of years you will be well aware of the implications for your business and industry. Use the information you have, and forecast the likely scenarios (using the scenario options analysis described later in this book) to build a picture of the likely effects on your business.

Political/legal/tax environment

It has been said that it is the task of organizations to find the best ways to achieve the outcomes they need. It is the function of those who frame laws and standards to set the rules that ensure organizations go about achieving those outcomes in a way that is acceptable to – and supports – society. Because the definition of 'what is acceptable' changes, and those changes can be embodied in the law or the way that tax is extracted, the forces that drive the constraints imposed need to be carefully monitored and understood. Attractive options can rapidly change, and marginally profitable businesses can be pushed under by politically inspired agendas. Your law firm, advisers or industry body should keep you up to date.

Economic environment

Like thousands of corks on an ocean, organizations rise and fall on the economic waves. Different industries bob about in different places – some closer to the crest, some deeper in the pit of the trough. Understanding where your industry is, where you are, and how you are likely to be affected by the broader economic swells, helps you to predict likely future demand, and provides a context in which you can make investment decisions.

Achieving this understanding is not easy. Any night of the week you can see an economist on TV predicting the future with a steely certainty... only to be proven wrong within a matter of weeks. I suggest you task a number of senior people in your organization to keep an eye on their own parcel of economic topic areas (some might do shares, some country performance/projections, some might track commodity prices, etc) and ask them to collect a range of opinions. They can share insights at executive meetings (which will probably immediately remove some of the tedium) and this will help you to keep a handle on what is happening.

Technological environment

Consider the magnitude of the changes driven by technology. What used to cost a pound to buy over the counter now costs less than a penny over the internet. Where workers used to have to physically travel into work they can now dial in from anywhere in the world. What used to be independent businesses now become linked as virtual companies. Everyone knows how much technology has affected every organization in the past 10 years (just look at the rapid migration from 'shopping in person' to 'shopping online', or the impact of e-books on bricks and mortar bookstores, or social media on marketing). The next decade may bring changes of equal magnitude. You need to look for signs of technological change that will become available, and the changes you will be obliged to make. Ask your IT person to report back on where the technology frontier is going – or any teenager.

Demographic environment

We are entering into uncharted waters. Never before has the world's population been so large, never before have we had this percentage of people in retirement as a proportion of the working population, never before have people lived for so long. The greying of the Western countries, the move from the country to towns and cities, and the inequitable spread of young people is a challenge for governments around the world. Perhaps the greatest. Perhaps even greater than climate change. It is a problem without a clear solution, and it is an issue that attracts too little public debate.

For your organization this could be a significant driving force for your future development (very possibly you could benefit if you properly understand the trend). Collect all the available information, have a talk with a few people who are looking ahead for your industry, and assess the likely impacts of demographic change on your business.

Social environment

Social trends influence buyer behaviour. These trends emerge and exert a force surprisingly quickly. Look at how the rising generation of computer-savvy, entertainment-oriented, well-educated workers is changing the shape of what being employed is all about... and what organizations have to deliver before they are satisfied.

Look at how social media (Facebook, Twitter, YouTube, blogs, etc) have changed how people communicate and how we get all kinds of information – even our news. These trends tend to be driven by the younger members of our population, so stay in tune with where this generation spends their time and money, and what they are talking about.

Create a summary report for each of the six environment areas. Each report should be presented as a three-column table – past, present, future; see Table 6.1. Note down the key features under these headings, and highlight the most important changes that your organization is likely to face in the next three to five years.

TABLE 6.1 Environmental analysis

Past	Present	Future

Barriers to entry analysis

Some organizations have to make a considerable investment in technology, equipment and premises before they can produce their first product or deliver their first service. This investment can be so great that it will deter all those competitors who are unable to, or are not prepared to, wait for several years to achieve a return.

Those who are existing players have the capacity not only to produce products, but also to dominate the distribution channels, tie up the available customers through contracts, secure future business through integrated systems, or lock out competition through some other means (such as warranty clauses) so that customers will incur a cost if they take their business elsewhere. These are barriers to entry. There are other barriers like licences, brand strength and a network of relationships.

You need to be absolutely clear about the extent to which your business is protected by barriers that make it difficult for a competitor to take your customers. If there are few barriers you will be vulnerable to others picking off your best customers, and so you need to cement your relationship in every way available.

Make a list of the barriers that protect your business. This list fills the first column in the three-column table shown in Table 6.2.

In the second column note the cost required for a competitor to break a barrier and compete with you. Take into consideration the changes it will need to make to its processes, products/services and people, as well as intellectual property that needs to be acquired/developed and sales hours in getting started. This figure will not be precise; it only needs to be a ballpark estimate.

In the third column note the likelihood that a competitor will be prepared to incur this cost. Make a separate list of the competitors who will make this

TABLE 6.2   Barriers that protect your business

Barriers that protect your business	Cost to a competitor	Likelihood that a competitor will make this investment

TABLE 6.3   Barriers that protect your competitors' business

Barrier	Cost to overcome this barrier	Likelihood of success

investment (if possible). Now, rank order this list with the most expensive barriers, with the lowest chance that a competitor will make this investment, at the top.

For completeness, you should also have a look at the barriers that your competitors are using to lock you out of potential customers. In the second column of Table 6.3 note the potential cost of overcoming the barriers. In the third column, assess your likelihood of success. You will have most of what you need in your potential customer analysis.

When you put these two pieces of information together you can see what barriers are in force, and which have the greatest strength. If there are few barriers that protect your business you may need to build stronger relationships with your customers to secure their business in the future.

Availability analysis

Some businesses may need to be located in a particular place (for example a specialist shop may need a position in a shopping centre). Others may need a steady supply of a particular raw material. The general availability of the features is a potential constraint. These can represent a barrier to entry, or a barrier to development, but are worth itemizing separately.

This is a straightforward analysis that can probably be completed relatively quickly. Create a three-column chart, like Table 6.4.

TABLE 6.4 Availability analysis

Requirements	Threats to those requirements	Likelihood of a threat becoming a reality

In the first column list the locations, equipment, raw materials and so on that you need to have available. Have a conversation with the people responsible for purchasing and other facilities (particularly floor space). In the second column note what will threaten that supply. You may need to look at global demand for a raw material, or you may need to look at local availability. In the third column quantify the likelihood that those threats will eventuate in the next three years. Use the 1–5 scale again. A score of 1 means that the threat is likely to become reality, 3 means that it is possible but not likely, and 5 means that the threat is remote.

Sources of information

You will probably have to ask in a few different places. Purchasing, property management, finance and sales will all offer information.

You have now gathered a lot of information about what is happening outside your business. Stand back from it all, and pick out the four or five key messages. The strategic process is starting to show you something about your business that you probably did not know before. Now it is time to lift the lid on what is happening inside your organization.

Go to **www.koganpage.com/editions/the-strategic-planning-workbook/ 9780749465001** and choose 'Understanding Pressure Points' for a video to accompany this chapter.

What are we thinking?

07

Understanding what is happening in your organization

Your strategy is going to be implemented by your people. How they think, what they do, what they value, what beliefs they share and how they organize their work will all impact on their capacity to make a great strategy work in practice.

Organizations are amazingly complex. This complexity is often underestimated and its effects are typically misunderstood. For example, consider the game of chess. How many possible moves are there during a single game – hundreds, thousands, perhaps millions? The answer is a staggering 10^{108}. That is 10 with 108 zeroes after it or, to put that another way, the time period from the big bang that started the universe to now – counted in seconds.

Now consider your organization. How much more complicated is it than a game of chess? In fact, how much more complicated than a game of chess is every job in your organization? If you don't acknowledge this complexity, then you can easily make the wrong judgements and deliver poor decisions.

> As the Chinese proverb says: 'The beginning of wisdom is to call things by their proper name.' (Confucius)

If you don't understand what is happening in your organization, then you will not be able to achieve your strategic potential.

So, you have this level of complexity that is interacting with, changing and being changed by other organizations and customers within a set of conditions and circumstances that are affected by many different variables. It is easy for managers to lose touch with the reality of where money is being made and lost and what is actually happening 'at the front line'. The bigger the organization, the harder it is to be sure that the picture that the managers have is current and accurate.

Try this simple test. Take a straightforward process that is completed by a lot of people in your organization over and over again every day. Ask the senior manager responsible for the area to draw a process map that describes how that process works. Now ask a supervisor to draw the map. Now select someone from the front line who actually completes the tasks and ask him or her to draw the process map. For good measure, observe the task yourself and draw your own map. What are the chances that those maps will be the same? What are the chances that the senior people will get a shock when they see how the task is actually done?

Process distortion is just one example of your organization's ability to develop and change in a way that is little understood. The same is happening in almost every part of your business. Typically it will happen invisibly because most measurement systems are designed to track the way in which money flows in the business for accounting purposes (which is interesting and important), but is not particularly useful as an indicator of what is really going on at a practical level, and what is likely to happen next.

In this chapter I will cover some tools that help you to understand how your business really works. These are:

- stakeholder analysis;
- culture analysis;
- skills matrix/talent analysis;
- financial performance analysis;
- process performance (using the sub-optimization analysis);
- risk analysis;
- resources versus outcomes analysis;
- cause and effect analysis;
- relative scale analysis (benchmarking);
- absolute scale analysis (using a framework); and
- change readiness analysis.

As mentioned before, these tools help you to gather clear information. The clearer the information, the easier it is to make decisions later on. Some decisions will virtually make themselves when you have all the data gathered in one place.

Stakeholder analysis

Stakeholder analysis is a tool to understand outside or inside groups. Usually it is a mixture of both, and I have included it with the suite of internal tools, although it could equally have been a part of the previous chapter.

Stakeholders are those groups that have a legitimate interest in your business. This interest can arise from supplying your business with products/services, benefiting from your products/services, working within the business, providing goods and services to those who work in your business, feeling the effects of your business (environment, community, etc), providing information about your business, regulating your business, owning shares in the business and so on.

To identify your stakeholders collect a cross-section of managers, a couple of senior administrative assistants and a couple of finance people (they know who your business deals with, and they often have good filing systems that point towards the stakeholder groups).

Ask this group to develop a list of stakeholders. Rake through this list a couple of times with the group to make sure that different stakeholders have not been put together under the same heading, or that the same groups have been allocated different headings. Now put the list in the first column of Table 7.1.

For each of the stakeholders ask the group to specify the following:

- The interest that this group has in your business (ie what makes them qualify as a 'stakeholder' in the first place), put this information in column two of the table.

- The needs of each group; this goes in column three. If you have any customer surveys or any other data of that kind, they will be helpful to this discussion. (It may be that there are several quite different,

TABLE 7.1   Stakeholder analysis

Stakeholder	Interest	Needs	Implication	Interrelationships

perhaps even conflicting, needs that start to appear. If this happens it is a signal that this group is a composite of several different stakeholders, and you need to create a different set of headings.)

- The implication of having these needs for your business; put this in column four. The question to ask here is: 'What do we need to do and what will it cost to meet these needs?'
- The interrelationships between the stakeholders; this goes in the final column of the table. So, for example, 'unions' and 'employees' may be separate stakeholders, but there is an interrelationship, or perhaps 'key customers' are also 'suppliers'. In this column list the other groups where a strong relationship exists.

Once this information is clear, ask the group to identify if the stakeholder is:

A A key player in the business, and their needs have to be largely/wholly met in order to generate success.

B A significant player, where perhaps all their needs have to be met some of the time, or some of their needs have to be satisfied all of the time, or perhaps they have the power to put significant barriers in the way of achieving success.

C A remote player, possibly one that is easily substituted for another, or can have little impact on your business.

Rearrange the stakeholder list, this time with the As at the top and the Cs at the bottom. This table now provides an initial analysis of your stakeholders. For some smaller businesses with a limited number of stakeholders, this level of analysis might be enough. However, if you have a more complex array of stakeholders, then you could gather more detailed information from one, several or all of these groups by using the techniques described in the customer analysis section.

This analysis is particularly important information for those in the public sector (or in public-sector like businesses) because the vision for the direction in which the organization will need to travel is to a large extent shaped by the needs of the stakeholders.

Culture analysis

What can you readily identify, but can't accurately define? What does every great business have that the 'also rans' in its industry do not? What is it that makes a business into a cult? It's the culture.

The culture that you wrap around people will not alter them as individuals, but it will influence their behaviour. It will shape the way they invest their energy, adjust their capacity to absorb change and affect their desire to do more than is expected.

Few people will argue that culture does make a difference, and in some industries it makes *the* difference. The trick to understanding culture is to appreciate that shared behaviour in organizations (the culture) does not come about because you teach people how to behave in a particular way. The behaviour is a consequence of a number of different drivers, which are:

- reward systems;
- the way that winners and losers are defined and treated;
- the example that is modelled by influential managers;
- where senior people place their emphasis;
- the nature of the work (particularly the degree to which tasks are mechanized);
- the organization structure.

Working on behaviour alone is unlikely to produce any sustainable change. It is the drivers that influence behaviour. If you want to change behaviour – change the drivers.

As part of this investigation stage of the strategic planning process it is essential to understand how your culture influences results today, and what limits it might put on your capacity to change in the future. You may have recently completed a culture survey that will provide you with the information you need. If not, then here is a shortcut to analyse the two characteristics that have a big impact on culture: fear and freedom.

Fear

Fear is a primary driver of human behaviour. To a greater or lesser extent we are all defined by our fears. Add a little fear into an organization and people stop taking chances, spend more time diluting responsibility in meetings, and introduce lots of checking steps.

If the fear persists (for years) then people become increasingly uncomfortable with even minor change. They displace anxiety in lots of activities that were never a high priority – such as developing complex policies for incredibly obvious issues, or investigating topics where there was already sufficient information. Typically this activity produces few ideas about how to change the situation.

Build an organization with low levels of fear and you will see the opposite. Here you will find creativity, full use of authority to get things done, all kinds of attempts to make changes, and probably some genuine breakthroughs.

Ask 10 people (from different levels in your organization) in two focus group sessions of 45 minutes each the following questions:

- What are people afraid of in this organization (losing their jobs, making a mistake, not getting pay increases, their managers, irate customers, etc)? How rational is that fear?
- How does that fear affect their behaviour?
- To what extent have the current managers developed this fear?

Within the answers to these simple questions are some of the insights that will help you to understand how the tone you set as a manager affects what people do every day. However, be very careful when you answer these questions, because culture is difficult to see from within. Ask someone who has just joined, as well as someone who has recently left, to get some different perspectives.

Freedom

Organizations are complex – we have already established that. People from supervisory levels upwards need to have the freedom to work within fairly broad guidelines so that they can get the required outcomes.

To be able to confer this freedom an organization needs to be confident it has the right people, the right information systems to support their decision making, and the right feedback systems to ensure that everything does not go off the rails. This freedom is only possible when there is a mixture of good design and interpersonal trust.

When people have this freedom, the organization finds ways around day-to-day problems and it is able to cater for new challenges and opportunities. When the freedom is absent, too many decisions are bounded by rules – which can never cover all circumstances – and so too many decisions end up in the in-trays of senior managers and do nothing but gobble up their time and slow down the whole organization.

The level of freedom available is easy to assess – just look at the restrictions imposed by the rules and levels of delegated authority. Interview five supervisors and five managers and ask them to describe the limits placed on their decision making, and what could be accomplished if their limits were increased.

Once you are clear about the degree of fear and the levels of freedom, then prepare two one-page reports. The first report should show the results of the fear focus groups. List the key findings for each group for each question. The second report should show the restrictions placed on decision making, with conclusions about the appropriateness of those limits. You are now ready to place your organization on the 'fear–freedom' matrix shown in Figure 7.1.

FIGURE 7.1   Fear–freedom analysis scale

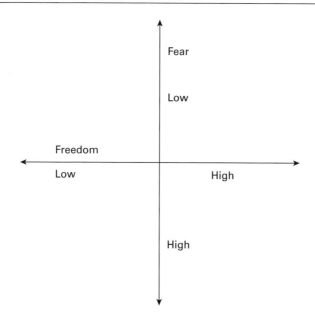

Take a look at your findings. Assess the answers for the freedom data on a scale that shows high freedom (fully responsible and able to make all necessary decisions), medium (key decisions not available) and low (needs to refer even the most trivial decisions). Then assess the degree of fear on a three-point scale – high, medium and low. High means that people are afraid of making changes, offering ideas, holding a different viewpoint from their manager, and are concerned about losing their job. Low means that there is little use of hierarchical power, everyone feels safe to express their views and experiment with new ways to achieve results, and they feel that their jobs are secure. Medium is in between.

Now place your organization on the four-quadrant scale. Your position on the quadrant tells you what shared behaviours are likely to be present in your organization:

Low fear + high freedom = innovative, accepting of change, experimental.

Low fear + low freedom = frustration, challenges to authority, rules will be broken.

High fear + high freedom = upward delegation, meetings to share decisions, low innovation.

High fear + low freedom = dependence on rules and precedents, resistance to change.

Any kind of recent culture/climate study should provide you with some useful information. Also, you could look at any recent customer study, particularly any information about responsiveness or flexibility, which will give you some clues. Another way to gain an insight into your culture is to ask those people who have recently joined – particularly if they have come from an organization that is seen to have a progressive culture. They will be able to list immediately what they found surprising, disappointing and in need of change.

Skills matrix/talent analysis

The culture analysis shows you how your organization gets work done. The skills and talent analysis shows you what the people in your organization can do.

People – particularly senior managers who are on a mission – often forget that an organization has a limited basket of knowledge and skills. It may be that your organization simply does not have the depth of skills to do certain kinds of work, and it may not have the spread of talent to be able to do much beyond the current level of complexity.

You may already have a skills and talent audit. If you do, you can add this to the pile of data that you are accumulating as part of the strategic planning process. If not, a full analysis of skills and talent is a significant piece of work. It involves identifying the competencies you need in your business and the extent to which each person possesses them. A talent assessment involves identifying who has the capacity to progress beyond their current level, and by when.

If you have not completed this kind of analysis, the best way to gather some indicative data is to ask the managers in your organization to make explicit what they must be thinking and talking about anyway. The process is as follows.

First get an organization chart. For this exercise, only consider middle and senior managers. This group is usually the hardest to recruit, and they are often the most specialized – and therefore the most inflexible. Use this chart to record information. Ask your human resource people or senior managers to help provide you with information.

You need the answer to two questions: what percentage of the knowledge and skills that this person needs does he or she actually possess today, and what percentage of the knowledge and skills that the person is likely to need in the future does he or she possess today?

FIGURE 7.2 Skills and talent analysis

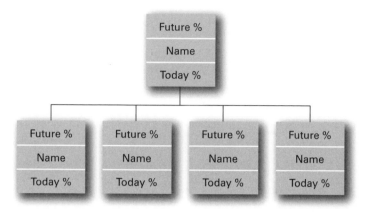

Once you have this for all the people on your charts – or at least a representative sample if you are a big organization – enter the figures. Using a chart like the one shown in Figure 7.2, place the percentage that represents today below the box with the person's name, and place the percentage that represents the future above. Circle any percentage that is below 80 per cent.

Now ask the third question: how many levels above his or her current level is this person capable of achieving in the next five to seven years: a) 1 level, b) 2 levels, c) 3 levels, d) 4 or more levels? Colour code the four options for potential by colouring in the whole box. Choose a different colour for each assessment (a–d). If the person is not going anywhere, then leave the box uncoloured.

This block of information has been built on the perceptions of managers from their direct reports rather than through a more formal system. However, it is likely that it will be no less than 75 per cent accurate, and as long as this limitation is remembered then this data highlight the realities that need to be considered later in the strategic process.

Sources of information

Any form of skills audit, training needs analysis, aggregation of performance appraisal data, bonus payment data or information about relative remuneration rates may either provide the information that you want or provide clues.

Financial performance analysis

This is the analysis that you are most likely to perform with the minimum of effort. The people in your financial/accounting function probably have the data already for regular monthly and annual reporting requirements.

The nature of the information that you will need to present will depend on the nature of your business. Whatever data you collect, I suggest you make sure that it includes the following:

- profit by product/service;
- margin by product/service;
- return on sales by product/service;
- performance against budget by product/service;
- return on assets for each division; and
- overall overhead costs for each division.

The data that you gather should be presented as a series of bars or plot points on a graph, like Figure 7.3. The data should begin two years before the most recent month, and there should be a bar/point for each month. You should also show budgets and forecasts on the same graph. This data should be arranged so that all the items that relate to a product/service are placed on the same page.

This spread of data may replicate your management information reporting. If this is new data, then you may well find that there are some surprises.

FIGURE 7.3   Financial analysis

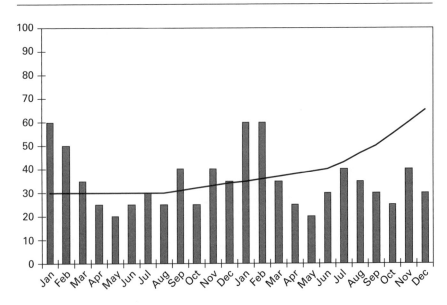

Most of this will reside in the finance function, or they will know how to find it/ calculate it. If there are missing pieces, then it is likely that the managers responsible and/or the sales area will keep their own records.

Process performance (using the sub-optimization analysis)

Process performance can be assessed in many different ways. I suggest you use the sub-optimization analysis – which is another one of my favourite tools because it is robust, flexible and always brings interesting data to light. (More detail on this and how it can springboard success can be found in my book *The Third Principle: How to get 20% more out of your business*, available from **www.lakegroup.com.au**) The research for this book showed that every organization is sub-optimized... guess by how much. If you picked that organizations are optimized by 20 per cent, then that is the figure I found in best-practice organizations. Ordinary/common practice organizations are sub-optimized by up to 60 per cent. Where do you think yours would fit in that range?

Select the five most important processes in your organization. Then create a clear picture of the optimized state for each one. The optimized state is where all the components of the process work as well as they could (and should), when everyone performs close to the levels exhibited by your best workers, where all processes are as sleek and free of defects as your best processes, where all customers are as profitable and trouble-free as your best customers, and so on.

So, let's focus on processes. Imagine how optimization would affect the measures that you have (such as sales, profit, waste, rework, turnaround time, and so on). This is the effect of being optimized. Enter this information next to the tall bar on the right-hand side of the graph in Figure 7.4, below the heading 'Key measures'.

Now consider the current situation. Using the same measures that you used to describe the optimized state, record the real situation in your business next to the short bar. What is the gap between current activities and outputs, and possible performance? Or to ask the question another way, how close are you to the optimized state?

FIGURE 7.4   The sub-optimization analysis

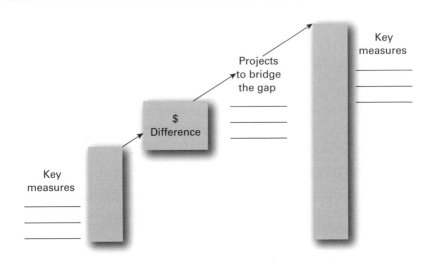

Calculate the consequence of being where you are by adding up the money you would have made if you were optimized, and the money you are making today. Enter this figure in the box provided. When you perform this calculation make sure that you include the costs that you are carrying because you are sub-optimized, as well as the opportunity cost – which is the business you did not get because you were tied up dealing with sub-optimization.

The chances are there is a considerable gap. This represents a considerable amount of money. It is also highly likely that this exercise has prompted you to see your business from a different perspective. Almost all management theory (and consequently management practice) is based on two organizing principles – efficiency and effectiveness. While these are important ways to view your business, they do not lead you to compare what you do now with the optimized state.

This straightforward tool forces you to ask another question and view your business in a different way. This is the time to list what kinds of projects you need to complete to take you from your current state to your optimized state. (This may well be a different list from the projects that you are currently pursuing – because you arrive at them from a different starting point.) You should note these in the 'Projects to bridge the gap' column.

Risk analysis

There is a whole industry built around risk analysis, particularly insurable risks and legal risks. The risk analysis that you need for this strategic planning process is more humble than the risk analysis you probably have for parts of your business, and concentrates on the possible impact of likely risks for the future. Consider these questions:

- What is the greatest risk you face with your customers?
- What is the risk that will most significantly affect your processes?
- What could your competitors do that would cause you the greatest harm?
- What risk do you run with your people?
- What risks are there with your premises and equipment?

For each of these risk areas develop a four-column table, like Table 7.2.

TABLE 7.2   Risk analysis

The risk	Impact	Consequences in lost profit $	Likelihood

In the first column list the risks that you face. These should be risks that are possible, not 'a comet hitting the earth' kind of risk that is not only remote (we hope!), but also difficult to plan for. The risks should be of sufficient magnitude that they will noticeably affect your organization, and are likely to occur in the next one to three years.

The second column shows the impact if the risk was to turn into reality; this is a narrative section that should contain a few words to explain the impact. The third column estimates the consequences of the risk in terms of lost profit over a one-year period.

The fourth column is an estimate of the likelihood that this risk will happen. If the likelihood is high then allocate a 1, if it is possible then allocate a 3, and if it is remote then allocate a 5.

Sources of information

If you don't have a risk manager, this analysis can probably be completed by asking those people who have been involved in developing your insurance requirements, and a good place to start is the accounts department. If the data do not exist, ask the managers of the areas that would be most affected. The chances are they have already considered the risks and effects. You will also find some of the data you need in some of the analyses you have already completed.

Resources versus outcomes analysis

In most organizations there are projects, activities or products/services that do not justify the time and resources invested in them. These may have been important at one time but are no longer relevant, may have been a good try that did not work, or may be an expression of a senior manager's ego. These investments sap your organization's finances, and they take people away from more useful pursuits.

The best way to reveal these organizational impostors is to list the projects, key activities and products/services that consume measurable amounts of time and/or resources. This list is the first column of a three-column table; see Table 7.3.

In the second column write down all the costs associated with the items on the list. These costs should include time, material, equipment, rent, management time invested – everything. Calculate the amount of money spent in the past 12 months.

In the third column write down all the outcomes this expenditure produced over the past 12 months. This should include sales revenue, costs

TABLE 7.3 Resources versus outcomes analysis

Projects/activities/ products/services	Costs	Outcomes

saved and any opportunity that was made possible. Possible future sales should not be included because they have not happened yet. This is about what has been delivered so far.

This information can now be transcribed on to a four-quadrant grid, like Figure 7.5, that shows which items have a low cost + high payoff, low cost + low payoff, high cost + high payoff, high cost + low payoff. Those that are expensive and return little will need special attention later in the strategic process.

FIGURE 7.5 Cost versus payoff analysis

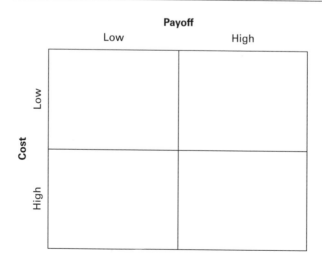

Sources of information

If you have some form of activity-based costing system there should be codes for identified pieces of work, so you simply have to collect or request reports. If there is no tracking system like this it is very hard for one person to gather this data. The best approach is to ask each manager responsible for an item on the list to specify the costs and outcomes and to perform the calculations. They are the closest to the information and probably have some records.

Cause and effect analysis

In a complex, messy system like an organization, bottlenecks choke work-flows, broken processes limp along unattended, the urgent problems get in the way of important priorities and interpersonal conflict masquerades as business practices. Too often these problems are invisible. Too often those closest to the problems cannot identify them for what they are, and cannot see the effects that are produced.

You know that these kinds of problems exist in organizations. You know this because an activity that requires 40 minutes of processing time in total (and therefore should be turned around in half a day at the most) can spend 30 days locked up in processes that recycle the same activity over and over again, and leave it in queues for days. You can see the human toll on the managers who lug home briefcases full of work every night, while those who work for them spend hours each day in non-value-adding activities. You know that the organization costs more than it should, but the source of the leakage is not obvious.

The cause and effect analysis is a simple way to bring to the surface some of the causes of the problems that are holding you back, but which no one can easily identify. This is not the same as the Ishikawa (fishbone) analysis that those involved in quality management will be familiar with, but a differently structured version which goes by the same name; see Figure 7.6.

The first step is to select a sample of people who work on those processes that are fundamentally important to the organization and which consume a lot of resources and/or people. This sample should include people at the front line, supervisors and managers. Organize these into three groups.

The second step is ask each group independently to identify what really gets in their way of doing a good job, and what really frustrates them. List their comments on a whiteboard, and ask them to perform an ABC analysis. This is as simple as it sounds. Ask the group to look at the list and identify which five represent the greatest annoyance – these are categorized as A,

FIGURE 7.6 Cause and effect analysis

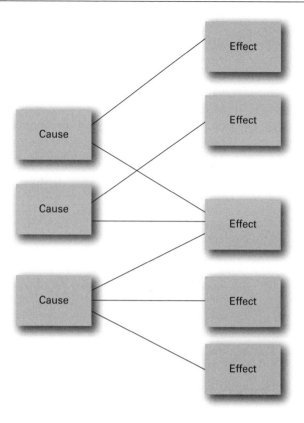

the second five categorized as B and the rest as C. That is all you need from each group.

The third step is to take the outcomes from each group and make a simple card for each of the A and B items mentioned. To do this you will need to consolidate the lists, so that where the groups used different words to describe the same form of annoyance you will need to pick a word that describes what they meant. Each different form of annoyance should have its own card.

The fourth step is to meet with some of the participants again. You need to consolidate the three groups into one by choosing the most insightful people you met from each. Invite these to a follow-up workshop. In this workshop lay the cards out on the table and ask them to identify which cards belong together. Typically people will be able to form clusters without too much trouble. Ask them to find a way to describe the common theme that unites this cluster of cards. Create a name for each cluster that summarizes what it is about.

Now ask them to identify any of the items on the cards/clusters that cause some of the others to happen. Lay the cards out on the tabletop – or on the floor if you need more room – so that the causes come before the effects. Link which causes produce which effects using pieces of string. While this may sound a bit like playschool, managers find it fun. Ask if there are any other causes that produce the effects that are represented on the remaining cards. Make new cards if you need to.

You now have a small group of cards representing the key causes of the difficulties people experience. If the people and process involved in this analysis are relatively typical, then they tell the story of the kinds of causal problems that probably blight the whole organization. This is usually very, very interesting.

Sources of information

This analysis relies on the knowledge of the people who work on the processes. Typically people know when something is wrong, and using this analysis framework can identify the issues giving rise to the problems – even when they could not have articulated the causes successfully in isolation. Supplementary sources of data include any process maps, process performance data or internal audit reviews.

Relative scale analysis (benchmarking)

Benchmarking is one of the most useful and one of the most poorly used ways to understand an organization. There are two main types of benchmarking: process benchmarking and end metric benchmarking.

Process benchmarking

Process benchmarking involves comparing how your organization completes the steps in a specific process with an organization that is seen to be world best at the same process. This enables you to learn and change.

To do this you need to pick a process that is critical to your business which you have already improved to the greatest extent possible within your own organization. Now find an organization that is world best at this process (this organization may be out of your industry – which is better because a competitor will not readily share what they have learnt with you) and ask if you can process benchmark. If you are lucky you will gain a favourable reply, and you can spend a delightful couple of days watching your process experts talk with their process experts about what could be different. A good time will be had by all and the learning can lead to a step change in your organization.

End metric benchmarking

End metric benchmarking is when you compare overall performance statistics – such as cost per unit, delivery times and so on – with other organizations. If you have different end metrics this causes you to ask questions.

Before you start to gather this information you need to be clear that different end metrics cannot be used as a performance table. It is data that provokes questions: it cannot confirm if your business is performing well (this is a trap that many organizations fall into).

The reason you cannot create a performance table out of benchmarking data is that some of the differences may be completely unavoidable (such as those driven by demographic, geographical or climate considerations), some may be unacceptable (your competitor may be happy using child labour in developing countries) and some may be caused by a variable that is distant from the process you are studying, but still has an impact (maybe an IT system). If you keep this trap in mind, collecting benchmarking data opens the door to carefully considering assumptions about your processes. There are three ways to gather benchmarking information:

1 internal benchmarking;
2 industry benchmarking;
3 generic benchmarking.

Internal benchmarking

If you are part of a large organization, with sites and plants all around the world, you may want to start by considering your current key performance indicators that show how each of these sites performs, and to highlight those sites that have the most favourable outcomes. This internal benchmarking will prompt you to list what it is that they are doing differently, and you can then identify what you might be able to incorporate into your processes.

If internal benchmarking is not available then you can go straight to comparing yourself with other organizations.

Industry benchmarking

Industry benchmarking relies on a significant number of players in the same industry sharing accurate data. This does not happen in all industries, so this kind of benchmarking is not always available. Also be careful of industry data, because some industries recycle the same people, the same concepts and the same mistakes. Being no worse than everyone else in an industry that is poor at, say, customer service, is a piece of information that is likely to mislead rather than enlighten.

Generic benchmarking

Generic benchmarking – that is, comparing yourself against world-best organizations that complete the same kind of processes – will often bring to the surface some interesting information, and may cause you to fundamentally re-examine and rethink your processes.

The best way to gather generic benchmarking data is to pick a small number of processes that are critical to your organization. Make sure you have good information about their current levels of performance. Approach your own industry bodies, professional associations and any place that looks after pooled data. They will probably have access to 'world best' data, or will know where to find it. If that draws a blank, try searching the web for benchmarking organizations (enter 'benchmarking' and you will find a list). From these sources you should find either the information that you need, or a good starting point. However, if you are still stuck, contact those organizations that you most admire and ask if they will share the statistics that you want. Typically each organization that offers data will want a copy of the report you produce – but beyond that many organizations are remarkably willing to share.

You can now list the processes that you have selected on a three-column table; see Table 7.4. Show the figures that represent your levels of output and then show how these compare with your benchmark partners. If there is more than a 15 per cent difference, then highlight this figure.

TABLE 7.4   Benchmarking analysis

Process	Your metrics	Internal/external (generic) metrics

Absolute scale analysis (using a framework)

Another way to assess your organization is to compare a set of your key features against a standard scale. The scales have been built by quality organizations and some specialist consulting firms. Unlike benchmarking – which shows you how you compare with other organizations – this assessment gives you a position on a scale against a set of criteria. These criteria represent the universal ingredients that are necessary in the recipe that will deliver organizational success. They typically include:

- leadership;
- people;
- policy and strategy;
- resources;
- processes;
- customers;
- impact on society; and
- business results.

There are several different ways to conduct an analysis. The most straightforward is to complete a self-assessment. This can be done in a formal way by gaining accreditation from the supplier of the scale and then going ahead and completing the analysis. Alternatively, if time and budget are against you, there are questionnaire-based surveys that give a broad indication of where you stand. Some of these are available on the internet.

The best way to present the data is to show where your organization stands on each scale, and then to highlight what low scores might mean for your organization. You could use a seven-column table for this analysis, like Table 7.5.

The first column contains the factors used by the scale you have chosen. The next three columns show the scores you have achieved. You could have a single column and simply record your score. However, by using three columns it quickly becomes apparent where your strengths and weaknesses are.

TABLE 7.5   Absolute scale analysis

	High score	Medium score	Low score	Implication	Action	Value
Leadership						
People						
Policy and strategy						
Resources						
Processes						
Customers						
Impact on society						
Business results						

The fifth column should be a brief summary of the implications of that score. This summary should be a few words only, and apply equally to both high and low scores. The sixth column is a summary of the kinds of actions these implications lead to, and the seventh shows the value of taking the action. At this stage this does not need to be a detailed calculation. Judge if the value is likely to be high (H), medium (M) or low (L), and use these letters in the seventh column.

Sources of information

There are several suppliers of these scales. You will also find that some of the benchmarking organizations may have information, and there are specialist firms that conduct reviews against similar scales. You may also find free questionnaires on the web.

Change readiness analysis

The world is changing. Your industry is changing. Your business is almost inevitably changing. It is likely that as a result of developing your strategic plan you will make some changes, and it is highly probable that some of these will be significant. As part of the pool of data you are collecting to fuel these changes, you should gather some data about how enthusiastically these changes will be greeted, and how well you are likely to manage the change process.

Change management is a whole topic on its own – and we will come back to this later in the book. For the moment, ask 10 key managers to fill in a completely confidential 'yes/no' questionnaire as follows:

The CEO is 100 per cent behind this strategic process	yes/no
This commitment will not waver in the face of opposition to the implementation plan	yes/no
We have managed change successfully in the past	yes/no
This organization is growing, so everyone is confident that anyone who is displaced will be found another job	yes/no
There are no pockets of sub-optimization, so no one will feel that some kind of embarrassing truth will come to light	yes/no
We do not have too many managers	yes/no
We do not have the wrong kinds of managers	yes/no
There is no concern that the strategic process will lead to a change that will produce 'winners and losers' amongst managers	yes/no
We have the time available to invest in making change	yes/no
The managers have the necessary skills	yes/no
The front line has the necessary degree of flexibility	yes/no

If all these statements score an unqualified 'yes', then changes will probably be relatively easy to implement – and you will be in a tiny minority of businesses. However, if you get 'no' answers to some of these statements, then you will have change management problems. The advantage of having this data early is that it tempers the speed and boldness of the change you will design.

If you wanted to enrich the data, you could use a scale of 1 to 5, with 1 representing a mild problem, 3 representing a mid-level problem, and 5 indicating a severe problem.

Sources of information

For this data it helps if the person making the judgement has seen (at least some of) the data collected in this strategic process. You might like to involve those key managers who have been in some way involved so far.

Another way to generate the data is to keep the set of questions listed above until the first strategic workshop and ask all those attending to give their opinions immediately after the data have been presented.

You probably have more facts about your organization than have ever been assembled in one place before. You have a lot of data – too much data. The next task is to boil this down so that the implications are obvious, and the actions are evident. You are going to do this with your executive team, in the next chapter.

Building the guiderails for the future
Mission, vision, values and measures

08

So, we have decided to put a proposal in for that project in Italy. This is, of course, completely in line with our vision to be the leading business in this industry... or was that to service the leading companies in the industry... or was that to attract the leading people in the industry... Anyway, I am pretty sure that going for this project is in tune with our vision... or was that our mission?

You have gathered a lot of data. This data tells you about the problems. It announces opportunities. It screams out for you to make the changes that will secure your future. Now you need to translate facts into information, information into decisions, and those decisions into actions.

Before you start you need to consider if you want to run a mission, vision and values workshop. To some extent people expect a strategic process to include the development of mission, vision and values statements. These three brief collections of words can gobble up a whole weekend retreat with the top team all by themselves. The results of this two-day investment can often confirm that the organization has a vision to be the best of its kind, a mission to delight customers and shareholders, and values that prominently feature respecting people and contributing to the community.

These are all worthy statements and sentiments. The thinking that produces them is the result of a useful exercise in getting executives to search their souls (or in some cases search for a soul) and to prioritize what they want.

However, it is extremely easy for the real meaning to get lost. Too often the precision needed is sacrificed to find the passion. Too often the passion that is felt is diluted and reframed into bland statements. Too often the statements are presented in a way that makes them difficult to use as business tools and hard to communicate. Too often printing key words on posters, mugs and mouse mats substitutes for real communication. In the long run all this does more harm than good, because it signals to the rest of the organization that the senior people are out of touch with the real world, and employees and customers are presented with a slogan when they really need a crisp definition.

If your organization already has a clear mission and vision and if it already has a core set of values that are well understood and are evidenced every day, then you do not need to read the rest of this chapter. However, if your strategic information gathering has shown you that you will need to fundamentally rework and rethink your organization, then spending some time working through the elements in this chapter will lay the right foundations for all the changes that are to come. I have covered:

- the shape that these statements should take;
- a structure that enables you to develop them (the workshop);
- a system for making sure that each one is reinforced every day.

The shape of the statements

Of all the areas in strategic planning, this is the one where it is easiest to get the concepts muddled up and to find mission, vision and values statements turning into hybrids that become a confusing collection of wishes, ideas and boastful statements about past achievements. So, let's make sure that we have the conceptual landscape completely clear.

Consider the picture in Figure 8.1 (we saw this earlier in the book), which describes the four basic choices available to any business. The choices are:

1 Stay the same, and get better (improve).
2 Stay the same, and get bigger (replicate).
3 Keep some parts the same, and introduce parts that are different (evolve).
4 Become substantially different (reinvent).

FIGURE 8.1 Four choices

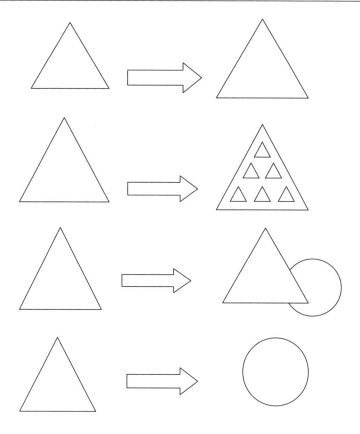

To describe your choice to your employees and other stakeholders you need to know the following:

- Where you are now – which is covered by
  - a clear picture of why your organization exists (the mission statement), and
  - where you are up to (the strategic research).
- Where you are going – which is
  - based on your research and strategic decisions, and then
  - captured in your vision statement.
- How to get there – which is described by
  - the detailed plan, which specifies what you need to do, and
  - the values statement that defines how you will go about your work.

So, the mission, vision and values statements are vessels for different types of information to be used to influence decisions and channel effort in your business. They each have a different job. Let's have a look at these in more detail.

The mission statement

The job done by the mission statement is to answer the question 'Why are we here?' Anyone should be able to read your mission statement and understand:

- what your business does;
- what customers your business serves;
- what makes your business unique.

These statements should relate to the enduring characteristics of your business that are likely to remain constant over time and represent the 'core' of what you are all about. So, to use a fictitious but illustrative example, consider the different types of businesses involved in the tea industry. The tea grower might have a mission statement something like the following.

> We grow the finest tea leaves in India for bulk sale to a select few processors. We own some of the best land on the banks of the Brahmaputra River, which is acknowledged as providing the soil and climate that produces the most densely flavoured leaves in the world.

The tea company that packages and then sells this tea to speciality stores may have a mission such as the following.

> We source the finest teas from around the world and mix unique blends for sale in speciality stores. We package these for the retail trade and our patented quick brew tea bags and snap seal technology provide the highest quality flavour retention in the industry.

The speciality store chain that sells the tea might have the following mission statement.

> We identify and sell the finest teas in the world to a) those customers who personally visit our shops and b) many more who are members of our web-based tea club. We are the sole provider of our famous propriety tea blends, which are among the most awarded and acclaimed teas in the world.

You can read these missions and instantly know what the organizations do. Just as important, those who work in the organizations and the customers who buy the products can understand why the business exists.

For any one of these businesses there would be a temptation to write a (so-called) mission statement that could sound like the following.

> We pride ourselves on our family atmosphere and values. Over our 50-year history we have continued to strive for quality in everything we do and we aim to delight each and every customer. We place great importance on ethical business practices and compliance with applicable regulations and policies, and we are committed to being an integrated organization with the needs of our shareholders and employees paramount in our decision-making processes.

This amiable – but meaningless – twaddle could apply to any of the tea businesses, or to none of them. If you have a mission statement that sounds even slightly like this one, then it is time to start again, because imprecision about why you are here means that you will find that all kinds of items that fall outside your 'circle of opportunity' will creep into your business and make it heavy and unprofitable. Your mission should defend the boundaries of your business, not act like a vacuum cleaner that sucks in anything that comes too close.

The vision statement

As we have already seen, there are four basic choices:

1 Stay the same, and get better (improve).
2 Stay the same, and get bigger (replicate).
3 Keep some parts the same, and introduce parts that are different (evolve).
4 Become substantially different (reinvent).

Your vision statement should be developed with the choice you have made, and its job is to answer the question: 'Where are we going?' All supervisors, managers, and executives should be able to assess their decisions against the vision statement and be able to identify if the outcomes they will achieve will take them closer or further away from achieving the vision.

For example, a vision statement that describes staying much the same, but getting better for, say, a niche manufacturer could sound like this.

> Following the outstanding success of our flagship product – the XP3 – it is our vision to work tirelessly to take performance of this unit to an even higher level by researching and developing the technology to fully automate both the operational and reporting components. Within five years the XP3 will be the component that will be considered to be essential in every computer in the world.

A vision statement for getting bigger for a university could be as follows.

> To service a rapidly expanding global market for quality higher education we will be the first European university to establish mega-campuses across the whole of Asia to offer our core curriculum in the local language and provide fully accredited international degrees. By 2020 we will be graduating over 20,000 students per year in this region.

A vision statement for keeping some parts the same and adding new parts for, say, a law firm could be like the following.

> Building on the current close relationships with the top businesses, over the coming years we will not only expand the capabilities of our existing practices and introduce new areas of specialization both domestically and internationally, but we will develop a full accounting practice and capability so that all our current and new clients come to a 'one-stop-shop' for all their professional needs. We will be the number one choice for at least 80 per cent of the first 100 businesses in the Fortune 500.

Here is a possible vision statement for reinventing a business.

Following the shift in technology from a tape to a digital medium we will use our considerable skills and expertise to reposition the business as an advisory group to help users to get the most out of the technology. Through the 'Institute of Digital Advice' we will run an increasing number of conferences and seminars both locally and internationally, and gain funding for research that will be available to both members (for free) and non-members (for a fee). We will become the global leader in providing advice about the practical application of the new technology, with a global membership surpassing 1 million within five years.

You will notice that these vision statements are specific and measurable. They have a five- to 10-year horizon and the reader is clear about what is planned to be achieved. Because they are so time-bound they will need to be revisited and possibly rewritten in response to emerging opportunities or changing circumstances. This is OK. In fact, this is the only way you can frame a vision that has true meaning for your employees and current or potential customers.

Don't be tempted to create a vision that has an enduring meaning, irrespective of what is happening in the world. The enduring statement is fine in theory, but in practice things change too rapidly for these types of statements to be able to continue to point you in the right direction. Typically the enduring types of 'visions' give you a nice warm feeling, such as 'To constantly surpass our customer's expectations' or 'To make the world a happier place', but these are really slogans that evoke an emotional response rather than describe where your business is headed. If you want a slogan (and it is a good tool to have), then call it a slogan and do not present it as a vision statement.

Also, your vision should be both grounded in reality and at the same time inspirational. If it sounds like 'To limp along and then fall in a heap', then you need to revisit the plans you have for your business. On the other side of the coin, if it has the flavour of 'To dominate the world', then you need to check if this is realistic given all the information you have about your business.

The values statement

The values statement is becoming increasingly important. Many organizations use their values statement as a reference point for decisions more than their mission or vision statements (although in some cases this might be because these statements are poorly framed). The job of the values statement is to answer the question: 'How do we go about doing our work?'

You may remember your history lessons where the army with the better 'morale' was able to defeat its better-equipped, larger, better-positioned opponent that lacked this ingredient. So it is with values. The business equivalent of this is the small research facility that finds breakthrough ideas ahead of the giant, lumbering, initiative-sapping R&D divisions, or the small sales team so ignited with passion that they take away the best customers from the tired market leader.

If your people possess, model and truly live the values that propel you towards success, then you are in a strong position to outperform your competitors. The values that underpin success cannot be copied from others in your industry or from best-practice organizations – they belong to your analysis of the kind of business you want to be now, and in the future.

It is not uncommon for similar sets of values to appear in many statements, values such as:

- customer orientation;
- respect for people;
- giving back to the community;
- ethical behaviour and integrity; and
- continuous improvement.

However, the interpretation and expected behaviours that fall under these headings may be – often are – different from one organization to the next.

Depending on the business – and to some extent where it is on its lifecycle – you may find other values that are clearly articulated and deliberately managed such as:

- risk taking;
- being entrepreneurial;
- acting with urgency;
- taking personal accountability; and
- inspiring others to act.

The mission, vision and values workshop

The mission, vision and values workshop is the activity that will help you to develop these statements. Each statement should be clear, crisp, brief and inspirational. The small number of words in each statement is not a reflection of the amount of time, effort and thought you will need to invest. Using the data that you have gathered during the strategic process, you can develop all three statements in one day with some or all of the executive team.

I have found that doing the vision statement first seems to work best. I am not completely sure why, but somehow the techniques makes instant sense for this statement, and then everyone cheerfully uses it for the rest of the day. Therefore, the three blocks for this workshop are:

1 creating the vision statement;

2 confirming the mission statement;

3 crafting the values statement.

Creating the vision statement

All the information you need is available. All of it is in the documents you have so far produced and in your executives' heads. The pieces of the puzzle that need to be assembled to make the statement you want are ready and waiting to be extracted. So, you have two tasks. You need to 'download' the information from the places where it resides, and then 'distil' it into a single statement.

For the vision statement you need to ask two key questions. The first is: 'Who has the right to set the vision for this organization?' The answer is not always obvious, so you may need to discuss this to make sure that you have identified the right individual/group. For example, it could be:

- the owner(s) of the business;
- the board;
- the CEO/executive group;
- the minister;
- the stakeholders.

If the group is in the room, then you can move on to the second question. However, if some of the group is absent (as is the case when the stakeholders set the direction – typically in a public-sector type of setting) then you need to bring their voice into the room. The way to do this is to look at the information collected in the stakeholder analysis. Allocate a couple of people to each stakeholder group and ask them to identify what that group really wants and needs your organization to become in the long term to meet their needs. Ask the people to summarize these expectations in a few words, and write each word down on a card.

The second question is: 'In the light of what is possible for this business, which key words capture the essence of where we are going in the future?' Break the executive team into smaller groups (of no more than four people) and ask them to choose the clearest, crispest, most informative and inspirational words that capture the essence of where your business is going. Write each one down on its own card (just tear an A4 page into quarters, to make four cards – this will do fine). If you are representing stakeholders, then complete the same exercise, but use the stakeholder cards you just created as a reference point.

You now have a number of groups with a number of words on cards. It is time for the first round of consolidation. To achieve this, combine the groups together, to halve the total number (so if you have six groups combine them into three, or if you have four groups combine them into two, and so on). The combined groups now have to distil the number of cards down to six. In some cases they will have the same words, but there will be a certain amount of debate about other cards.

When each group has six cards, choose five people to be the final decision makers (preferably people from different groups). While the rest of the executive team observe (but may not comment), these five people take the cards already generated and distil them further into no more than 10 key words. At this point they can combine cards to form a new word. When 10 cards remain, choose your best two wordsmiths and ask them to take the cards out of the room to a quiet place. Give them no more than 20 minutes to create a vision statement using the key words on those cards.

Confirming the mission statement

Creating cards is an amazingly powerful way to generate these types of statements. It is so powerful that we will use it again to confirm the mission statement.

You have already produced a lot of information about your business, its customers, its uniqueness, its strengths, and so on. Ask the executive to review the customer analysis, potential customer analysis, hallmarks of success analysis, relative and absolute scale analyses, and the lifecycle, portfolio and SWOT analyses from the decision-making workshop. Now, take them through exactly the same steps with the cards and the levels of consolidation. The only difference is that this time they are creating key words for three aspects of the mission statement, as shown in Table 8.1.

The first round of consolidation groups can produce six cards for each part of the statement and the final round can distil this down to 10 cards for each part. Once again, ask two people to wordsmith a definite and definitive statement that describes your mission.

Crafting the values statement

The card technique is working so well, and people are getting so good at using it, that we will use it again – but this time with a twist.

Put your freshly developed mission and vision statements onto sheets of flipchart paper and stick them on the wall. Break the executive into four

TABLE 8.1 Key words for three aspects of the mission statement

We provide:	
For:	
Our uniqueness is:	

groups and ask them to specify the behaviours that people need to evidence to be able to:

- sustain the mission from the internal perspective;
- sustain the mission from the external point of view;
- achieve the vision from an internal perspective;
- achieve the vision from an external point of view.

Again ask them to record each behaviour on a card. Make sure that they describe observable behaviours ('challenge authority figures in meetings') rather than feelings ('be happy').

When there is a complete list of behaviours (or as many of the key ones people can write in about 40–50 minutes), lay them all out as a single column (you will probably need to use the floor). First identify all the overlaps, and remove the duplicate or triplicate cards. Then identify the behaviours that seem to belong together, and put them next to each other. Now you are ready to identify values.

Looking at the clusters of behaviours you have in front of you, extrapolate back by asking the question: 'What values give rise to these behaviours?' Create a card for each value identified, and put these on the left of the clusters. When all the values have been identified, rearrange the clusters of behaviours so that they sit together next to the value that gives rise to them. If the same value produces more than one of the behaviours, signal this with a strip of paper, drinking straw or piece of string. If you have more than 10 values, look for mega-values that have your existing values as subsets, and bring these subsets together.

Now you have the values you need to be successful and a list of the behaviours you expect to emanate from those values. You can create a flip-chart list and ask your wordsmiths to create some connecting words and brief definitions. Good work.

Reinforcing the statements every day

'Customer service is absolutely critical to this business', said the CEO. 'Customer service is essential to this business', said the Regional Manager. 'Customer service is a priority', said the Branch Manager. 'Customer service is very important', said the Supervisor.

Mary heard/saw/read all these statements, but she knew what she had to do to get promoted. She knew what targets she had to achieve and what criteria she had to fulfil. None of them had much to do with customer service. So she kept on inflicting the same old experience in the same old way.

How do you make sure that something gets done in an organization? That's right... you measure it, and you make sure that the measure is important to the individual's personal success.

The mission, vision and values statements get traction when they are accompanied by measures that define the required outcomes, track performance against those outcomes, identify gaps, and stimulate remedial programmes. Now, building a full set of measures is a reasonably substantial project, but there is a short-cut you can take to help you identify if your measures are sufficiently comprehensive to support your strategic process.

Once again, you will run a one-day workshop (which could follow directly after the mission, vision and values workshop to make both into a two-day event). The key technique is the card sort (you are getting really good at this by now).

To begin, display the flipchart sheets with the mission, vision, and values statements. Then form your group into three sub-groups. Each sub-group will have either a mission, or a vision, or a values statement. Ask each group to consider the statement they are looking at and make a card for each measure that would need to be in place to be able to accurately assess if the outcomes expected by the statement are being produced. So, for example:

- If the vision included increasing market share, then there needs to be some measure(s) that describe the level of market share achieved by your business (in size, value, and so on) on a quarterly, six-monthly or annual basis (depending on your industry).

- If the mission included the word 'quality', then questions that will identify the types of measures you need are: 'What kind of quality?', 'To what level?', 'As measured by who?' and so on.

- If the values statement included the collection of behaviours that support 'innovation', then the measures you might need include the number or financial value of internal changes introduced each year, or the number or financial value of new products/customers, or the number of patents achieved and so on.

Point to every word in the statements and ask the question: 'How do you know?' For the moment do not worry if the information to fuel these measures is currently collected, or has never been collected, or may be difficult to collect. Keep on asking this question until every statement has a full list of measures.

Using a large area (probably the floor or boardroom table) make cards for the words 'Mission', 'Vision,' and 'Values' and put these cards a reasonable distance apart on the left-hand side of the area you are using. To the right of these cards lay out the measures you have just created as a column. Give everyone in the group the opportunity to have a look at the measures created, and allow people from different groups to ask questions and perhaps add other measures.

You will probably have a reasonably comprehensive list of measures, but to make sure that you have catered for all business activities, ask the whole group to list the other measures you need to run the business. It may be that some belong within the categories (in theory they all should, but sometimes there are a lot left over). Put these additional measures in their own category below the columns you have laid out.

Now, you need to complete a quick check to make sure that there is reasonable representation of different types of measure. Make four new cards – 'Processes', 'People', 'Customers' and 'Finances'. You will recognize these as being broadly compatible with the 'balanced score card' headings. These will serve as a horizontal axis and should be laid out above the columns you have created. So, you should now have a couple of axes that look like Table 8.2.

Ask the whole group to allocate the measures they have just created into this grid. There should be a representation in all boxes. This is unlikely to be evenly distributed (depending on your business, industry and ambitions) but if all the measures are clustered in a couple of boxes, or if there are completely empty boxes, then you should lead a discussion to make sure that proper consideration is being given to all aspects of the business.

This discussion may prompt the group to change or develop some of the measures. When you are satisfied that you have the right balance of measures, use four different coloured dots to colour code the measures so that you can tell if they are process, people, customer or financial measures.

You are now going to complete another type of analysis. Keeping the measures in their categories of mission, vision, values and other, collect them up and put them aside so you can set up another grid. Remove the 'Process', 'People', 'Customers' and 'Finances' headings and replace them with headings that say 'Level 1', 'Level 2', 'Level 3' and 'Level 4'. You should now be looking at a grid like the one in Table 8.3.

TABLE 8.2   Different types of business measure

	Processes	People	Customers	Finances
Mission				
Vision				
Values				
Other				

TABLE 8.3   Measures at different levels

	Level 1	Level 2	Level 3	Level 4
Mission				
Vision				
Values				
Other				

Level 1 measures are the ones seen by the CEO/executive/senior management level. They do not provide the fine detail in the business ('Did Mrs Smith get her product delivered on time?' type of stuff) but they do provide information about delivery performance (percentage of orders delivered on time and in full in the past quarter). Level 2 are the measures looked at by middle managers. Level 3 are for the supervisors. Level 4 are for the front-line people. It may be that you need to create fewer or more than four levels; simply adjust your cards to suit your circumstances.

Now take your measures and allocate them to the correct place on the grid. It may be that you need to make some duplicate cards, as the same measure applies at two different levels. If so, make sure that you decorate the new card with the right coloured sticker. It is also highly likely that you will have to make some new cards, as you will probably find that there are gaps as an item is measured at (say) levels 1, 3, and 4 but not at level 2. You may also find that measures apply at level 3 that are not aggregated up in any way to the level above. Do not be concerned about making too many new cards. Having too many measures that can later be trimmed is much better than having too few measures that mean that parts of the business are under-described.

Conclude the workshop by spending a few minutes placing a sticker or mark on those measures that you do not currently use in your business. These will become a project for someone to develop.

You now have a pretty reasonable measures framework for your business that will support fulfilling your mission, achieving your vision and living your values. Sure, it will need to be refined, and targets will need to be added, but once these measures are introduced you will have a way to make sure that the mission, vision and values statements are used every day to make your business as successful as possible. You are now ready to make some big decisions.

Go to **www.koganpage.com/editions/the-strategic-planning-workbook/ 9780749465001** and choose 'Mission, Vision and Values' for a supporting video for this chapter.

09

How to pick a strategy that is right for your business

The big day had arrived. Malcolm had collected all the data. He had enjoyed asking the questions, had been surprised by the findings and had received an extraordinary level of support. He should be looking forward to the workshop. He should be excited about the decisions that they were about to make.

But he wasn't. He knew how difficult some of the people could be. He had seen too many meetings fizzle out without gaining consensus. He was tempted to run away.

You have arrived at the point where you need to run a strategic retreat to make the key decisions that will deliver success to your organization.

Some of your managers may have been stung by an unhappy experience in a similar gathering. The reason for their disappointment is that too often these workshops are built on thin data, and are overcrowded with annoying techniques. While they produce lots of discussion, not enough reasoned argument takes place. The result is the painful combination of too few decisions, and too many action plans that quickly fizzle out.

However, you are going to run a spectacularly successful decision-making workshop. The reason is that you have compelling data. You are going to use that data as the foundation for discussions. You are going to use practical techniques that corral the conclusions into a shape that forces people to make good decisions.

The most senior team in your organization (or perhaps the division of your organization that is the focus of this planning process) will participate in these workshops. It must be the most senior team because:

- They are the best equipped to make sense of the data.
- They need to build the options.
- They need to understand why some options were rejected.
- They need to make the decisions.
- They all need to know why decisions were made.
- They need to identify the activities that will turn the plan into reality.
- They will be clear about how the whole plan fits together.
- Their participation means that they will be committed to making it happen.

There are several excellent techniques that help you to use your data to run a successful 'strategic retreat'. In this chapter I have outlined eight of the most practical and generally applicable. I have described how they work and what you should do with the outcomes. Before we look at the content of these techniques, I will cover some of the key aspects of facilitating the process.

Facilitation

Before you get too focused on the content, you should think about the process that you need to follow for this workshop. There are five workshop facilitation techniques that you should apply:

1 setting expectations;
2 managing status;
3 setting ground rules;
4 managing conflict; and
5 getting started.

Setting expectations

People will bring different expectations into the workshop. Until everyone understands what will be covered (and what will not), and their role in the workshop, you will not be able to focus the participants on the decisions they need to make. There are three ways to shape people's expectations:

- Send all the participants a set of the data you gathered in Chapters 2 and 3. Make it clear they need to have read this before they come. If you think some of them will not be particularly enthusiastic, task each person on the executive team to become an expert on two or three items of data. Tell them that you will call on them to explain what it means. This will ensure they read at least some of the material and (for some strange reason), if you have made them read a portion, they usually read it all. If you want to give them background on the strategic process then you could also include one or several of the articles from my website (**www.lakegroup.com.au**).

- At the beginning of the workshop outline the kinds of decisions the group will make during the course of the two days. Outline the agenda, but do not specify the timetable. (Managing time is your problem: you may choose to spend longer on some items and you do not want people in the room to fuss.)

- Ask if there is anything else people want to cover. If it is already included then explain where it appears on the agenda. If it is not included, see if you can accommodate it easily. If you can, do so; if you cannot, explain why.

Managing status

In the workshop you will have several layers of your organizational hierarchy. You need to make the status difference as invisible as possible – otherwise everyone will just do what the CEO says, and you will not get much useful discussion. Here are several ways to minimize the status effect:

- As far as you are concerned – as the facilitator – as soon as you enter the workshop room put aside all thoughts of the place you occupy on the organization chart. You are in charge, and these people will do what you say, when you say so. Everyone expects this, and will accept it. Do not allow the CEO or others to bully you.

- Make it clear that in the workshop room everyone is equal. Everyone has the right to say anything within the normal tolerance of politeness.

Participants are allowed to disagree – they are not allowed to be disagreeable. Also:

- Make sure that dress is casual. A CEO in slightly silly shorts is a good deal less intimidating than one in a designer suit.

- If the CEO or another manager is clearly dominating the discussion, thank them for their contribution but ask them to hold their comments until others have had a chance to offer their suggestions.

- Call on people by name if they are not being given much chance to join in, so that you get their thoughts.

- Break people into small groups to consider questions. That way you have to get more than one opinion.
- If you really want completely independently generated ideas, ask the participants to write their responses to your questions on a piece of paper, and collect these.

Setting ground rules

Right from the start you need to set some rules. There should be three rules about the way in which people offer suggestions/comments. These are:

1 Every comment should be supported by facts. For example, when people identify a weakness, they are obliged to find the items of data that provide the hard evidence which proves that the weakness exists. Facts fuel reasoned discussions.

2 The facts should be considered in the right way and at the right time. There needs to be a framework for discussing those facts so they are dealt with in the right order, and so similar information is presented together. You are in charge of the structure, and you will be ruthless about maintaining the programme that you have developed – or you will not be able to give each topic the proper amount of emphasis and consideration. Structure makes sense of complex sets of facts.

3 Decisions will be made at the right time and by consensus. It will be clear what decisions are required, and these will be made and put together in a plan that can be implemented. Information will provide the options, and logic will be used to select the best.

Managing conflict

Conflict is not a problem. You should expect disagreement. If there is no conflict then you have probably not stretched the executives enough, and you have not shocked them out of their comfort zones. However, the conflict needs to be resolved. There are three ways to achieve this:

1 Ask the people in conflict to specify those areas where they agree. Then ask them to specify areas of disagreement, and get them to identify how they could create a set of criteria that would make it easy to resolve the areas of difference.

2 If the individuals cannot agree, ask the rest of the group to offer solutions or to invent other options that might satisfy both. List these options and get those in conflict to choose one they both can live with.

3 If you are really stuck, ask the rest of the group to vote on a solution – and move forward.

A good reference point for resolving conflict is to reflect on customers' needs. Make sure that you take along those collages that you developed when completing the customer analysis. They should be at the front of the room at all times to serve as a touchstone for discussions.

Getting started

The way you start the workshop makes a really big difference. The first morning will establish the tone and flow of the whole event, so a good beginning is important.

Before launching into the analysis you need to get your group warmed up a bit. You do not want them worrying about saying something dumb. You want them to become more involved in saying something interesting. To do this they need to be relaxed and confident. This is the 'ice breaker' session, which is often done poorly.

There are lots of different ways to jump-start one of these sessions. I favour any technique that gets people to disclose something the group may not already know, for example:

- Ask people to give three 'facts' about themselves. Two need to be true, and one false. During the lunch/dinner breaks people have to find out from each other which facts are correct.

- Ask people who they would like to be (if they could be anyone in the world) and why. (I once had someone say that he would like to be his wife, so that he could live with himself.)

- Ask some direct questions, such as who represented their school in a sport, who likes certain kinds of music, and so on (the questions will vary, depending on the nature of your executive team).

All of this should be done in a fun way – you are trying to produce laughter and create a high level of relaxation and camaraderie straight away. The big determinant here is you. If you are really anxious you will infect the whole room (not wanting to put more pressure on you, but it is true). You can suppress your own nerves by being clear in your mind about the flow of the workshop, and knowing what you are going to say, and when. You can bolster your confidence by reminding yourself that you have completed all the required analysis, and that you are going to be doing the business equivalent of pulling a few rabbits out of a hat as you reveal the findings through the use of the tools. This is going to be impressive.

If your CEO/chairperson is going to open the workshop, ask him or her to do so after this icebreaker. Also allow a very limited amount of time, and try and do a rehearsal with him or her before the workshop. There is a form of madness that is common among some senior people that compels them to talk and talk and talk as soon as they get in front of a group of people. This is like a bucket of cold water on the atmosphere that you have just generated, and eats up your precious time. Make sure you give the CEO/chairperson a defined outcome, and a few key points that he or she should cover. If he or she has to use graphics to support the points, make sure that there are no more than five slides.

Once you have got the required results from the icebreaker (and survived the opening address), begin by writing the following words on the whiteboard.

> The real voyage of discovery consists not in seeking new landscapes, but in having new eyes. (Marcel Proust)

Let this sink in. Then explain how you are going to view the business through new eyes, so you can create the best possible future.

Now that you are ready to facilitate the retreat, let's consider the eight techniques that you will use.

The eight techniques

I have described techniques that you need for decision making in a 40-minute video that accompanies this book, which you can find on the Kogan Page website at **www.koganpage.com/editions/the-strategic-planning-workbook/9780749465001**. In this video you join me as I am running a strategic retreat for a group of managers at the Swiss Grand Hotel at Bondi Beach in Sydney. I hope you find it informative and fun. I recommend that you have a look at the video before you read the rest of this chapter. If you have a few spare moments I also suggest that you spend a little time on my website: there are some articles, shorter videos on strategic planning and related topics.

The eight techniques are:

1 Scenario options analysis
2 Market future analysis
3 Lifecycle analysis
4 Portfolio analysis
5 SWOT analysis
6 Concentration of effort analysis

7 The activity hedgehog

8 Movement analysis

The first three of these techniques help the executives to boil down the data they have so that it becomes useful information. The next three support decision making, and the final two help you to design the change programme.

I have written this chapter assuming that you are the facilitator of the retreat. I have imagined that you are in a room full of senior managers and that you have to present the data, stimulate analysis, encourage discussion, record the outcomes and ask the questions – so that decision making is easy. I have given you some hints about how to facilitate successfully, and I have described the techniques that you will need. In the Appendix I have provided you with a draft agenda for this event (see Worksheet 1).

I have threaded these techniques together with an explanation of how to present them. You will see that I have described the technique, and then provided you with a way to use it effectively with a group.

Scenario options analysis

Overview of the technique

'Would you tell me, please, which way I ought to go from here?'
    'That depends a good deal on where you want to get to', said the Cat.
    'I don't much care where', said Alice.
    'Then it doesn't matter which way you go', said the Cat.
                       (Lewis Carroll, *Alice's Adventures in Wonderland*)

The bulk of the information collected so far tells you what has happened in the past. You now know where there are areas of lost opportunity in the market, where sub-optimization is hiding in your organization, and where costs are too high for the benefits that you gain.

However, before you can develop a plan you need to make some assumptions about what the future will be like. You need to assess the extent to which your organization may need to change over the next three to five years and in what direction, so you can be sure the changes you are about to introduce will support your journey to the best future possible.

This is where scenario options analysis comes in; it helps you to answer the question 'What is likely to happen next?' This is not a full scenario planning exercise – that is an investment of several days of the senior managers' time and a separate block of analysis. This is about performing a quick and practical check to see if there are any nasty surprises around the corner.

How to use it with a group

Remind people that in the workshop you will be dealing in facts, not suppositions. Ask them to read the environmental analysis, the customer analysis, competitor analysis, hallmarks of success analysis, financial analysis, risk analysis, absolute scale analysis and the relative scale analysis. If you have asked some managers to become 'experts' on any topic, ask them to summarize their understanding. Once the group have covered the key points, and you are confident they have absorbed the contents of these analyses, you are ready to begin.

This is not an easy exercise to complete, because the group can easily get lost in the discussion. You need to keep the questions crisp, and need to stop the conversation from straying off the topic. Pattern your questions as follows.

'If you could project yourselves three to five years into the future, what is the likelihood that this organization would be exactly the same as it is today?' The answer to this question is, of course, pretty obvious. It makes sure everyone knows you are going to be making some changes to the business.

'Looking at the data you have, what are the biggest changes you will experience that will cause things to be different?' There will be a variety of different answers. On the whiteboard list the different types of changes people call out. They could be a rise/fall in price, the development/demise of products, change in customers/competitors, political/social developments and so on.

'Looking at this list, there are x (add this number up) different possible changes, and even more possible combinations of those changes. Which are the most likely to occur?' List the most likely. If there are more than six, ask the group to rank order these and keep the top six. Create six small teams and allocate them an option each. Ask each team to develop a list of: 1) the changes that will take place, 2) the responses your organization will need to make, and 3) the kind of organization you will become if you make those responses. Ask the team to invent a snappy title to describe the scenario. Also ask the team to record the early warning signs that let you know this possible future is beginning to happen. Record these on flipchart paper, stick them on the wall and reconvene the group.

Now say 'Here are the more likely futures that you will experience. Is there any evidence that one or more is starting to come true?' If so, list what is going on that tells you this is happening under 'Early Warning Signs'. It is likely that one or two of the future scenarios will have early warning signs. Your six flipchart pages will look like Table 9.1.

TABLE 9.1   Scenario options analysis

Possible future 1 (a) changes (b) your response (c) kind of organization you need to become Early warning signs:	Possible future 2 (d) changes (e) your response (f) kind of organization you need to become Early warning signs:	Possible future 3 (g) changes (h) your response (i) kind of organization you need to become Early warning signs:
Possible future 4 (j) changes (k) your response (l) kind of organization you need to become Early warning signs:	Possible future 5 (m) changes (n) your response (o) kind of organization you need to become Early warning signs:	Possible future 6 (p) changes (q) your response (r) kind of organization you need to become Early warning signs:

You now have a set of reference points that you can use to test the decisions you will make during the workshop.

This is a good exercise to begin with, because it gets everyone thinking about the future and it prepares them for the idea that they will be making decisions that will have a significant effect on your organization. It also forces them to read and work with most of the information that you have prepared.

Market future analysis

Overview of the technique

> Management is efficiency in climbing the ladder of success; leadership determines whether the ladder is leaning against the right wall. (Stephen Covey)

A market that used to provide you with lots of healthy profits may no longer hold the same potential. A market that once looked promising may turn out to contain less than expected. A market that you had not really considered seriously may offer more than you previously thought.

These changes happen in a way that is not always obvious. This analysis shows you which market is most favourable to your current products/services. You should also look at your potential customers in this analysis, so you can identify markets that you do not currently service.

As a result of this analysis the executive group may have to face the reality that some of the projects to enter new markets they have started in the past 12 months need to be wound down (a blow to someone's ego). It is better that they come to this realization in this workshop – rather than you being the bearer of bad news later on. When you have completed this analysis you will be able to answer two questions: 'Where are the market opportunities diminishing?' and 'Where are the market opportunities expanding?'

How to use it with a group

On the whiteboard draw a simple graph with profit on the vertical axis and time on the horizontal; see Figure 9.1. The time axis should include the past two years and the next three years.

Explain that you are now going to analyse what is likely to happen in the key markets in the future. Ask the group to review the information you have about customers, potential customers, barriers to entry, availability, competitor and financial performance analyses. Also ask them to look at the scenario options analysis that you have just completed.

Say to the group, 'List all the key markets that you operate in, and those that are possible if you were to gain your potential customers.' When this list is complete ask the group to highlight those markets that are really only

FIGURE 9.1   Graph to support market future analysis

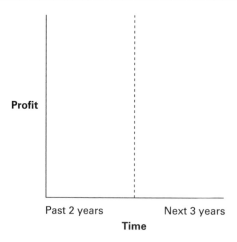

filled by one customer. If your business does not really operate in markets, but instead has a small number of large customers, complete the same exercise, using the customers as the focus of your attention.

Break the executive into small groups and allocate each group an equivalent number of markets/customers to work on. Ask the executive to sift through the information available, so they can replicate the picture you drew on the whiteboard or flipchart paper. For each market draw a line that shows the past two years (fact) and the next three (informed guess). For potential markets/customers they can only show the informed guess. These potential markets should be drawn in green, while the others should be drawn in blue. Collect up the charts, and stick them to the wall next to each other.

FIGURE 9.2   Key market analysis

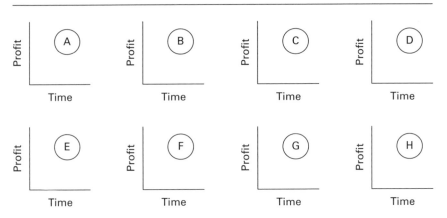

They show you two key items of information. The first comes from the direction of the arrows. If the blue lines are predominantly flat or pointing down, the markets you currently serve are stable or in decline. Profit in your business will be squeezed. This shows the need for the rapid acquisition and development of new customers, or the development of different pricing/ margins. In less than half an hour you could total the sum of the forecasts and show the level of future profit that is likely.

The second item of information comes from the industries/customers that show the same pattern of arrows. If all the customers of a particular kind or all the players in the same market are showing a decline in the profit you are expecting, you need to take a harder look at the attractiveness of continuing to do business with that group.

You can now see where the money is likely to come from in the future.

Lifecycle analysis

Overview of the technique

> Everything goes through a process of growth and decline. The dinosaurs, the Roman Empire, you and I – nothing is immune.

Every product/service has a lifecycle. Like a person, there is the birth where the product/service is full of promise and consumes amazing quantities of time and resources. There is a growth spurt in adolescence when it seems invincible, where rules do not apply and there is a feeling that the good times will always roll. Then there is the maturing of the product/service where costs have to be managed, where growth slows and where the best years are behind. Finally, there is the decline and ultimately the demise of the product/service. Unlike people, however, it is possible for a product/service to get reborn – particularly those in the fashion industry.

Products/services in different stages of the lifecycle produce different profit expectations and require different approaches from management. The early stages require funding and support; the growth stages are sustained by allocating your best people and by allowing experimentation and initiative; the mature years call for controls, the consolidation of processes, the formalization of decision making, the relentless pursuit of budgets and targets. The decline needs to be recognized when it comes, so resources can be withdrawn quickly before the profit made in the early years is eaten away.

Understanding where your products and services are in their lifecycle helps you to calculate how much value is left, and it foreshadows what is likely to happen next. This analysis helps you to answer three questions:

1 Which products/services hold the greatest promise?

2 Which products/services need to be managed in a different way to deliver profits?

3 Which products/services need to be scrutinized?

In the same way that the market future analysis shows what is happening outside your business, this analysis shows you what is happening to the products and services within.

How to use it with a group

Draw the basic lifecycle picture on the whiteboard; Figure 9.3 shows an example.

FIGURE 9.3 Life cycle analysis

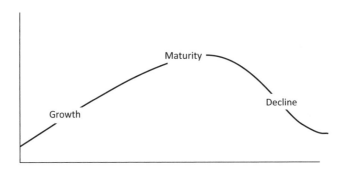

Explain the concept of the lifecycle, and make it clear that you are now looking at products/services and not markets/customers. If you have too many to readily manage, pick your top 20 per cent or so.

Ask the group to draw on data from the customer analysis, competitor analysis, financial performance analysis and relative data analysis. You can also use the market future analysis you have just completed. Ask them to list the products/services and potential products/services that should be considered in the workshop.

Break the executive team into smaller groups. Allocate an equivalent number of products/services and ask each group to draw the bell-curved life-cycle picture on a piece of flipchart paper and place a mark at the point where each of those key products/services is located. Once again, indicate potential products/services in red, and the others in blue. Stick all these pictures next to each other on the wall.

If you have a lot of mature or declining products you are an organization that may be depending on past glory, rather than deliberately trying to invent the products for the future. If you have few mature or declining products you are either an established business where the market just keeps on expanding, or you are relatively new and you need to start to develop the disciplines that will help you to cut costs so you can retain your margins.

Now you know which products/services will deliver you to future success, and from the previous analysis you know which markets/customers represent the best place to offer those products/services. Some of the decisions you are going to make are becoming a little clearer, but it is not time to make decisions just yet.

Portfolio analysis

Overview of the technique

> Charles Lamb's classic 1822 essay 'A Dissertation on Roast Pig' gives a satirical account of how the art of roasting was discovered in a Chinese village that did not cook its food. A mischievous child accidentally set fire to a house with a pig inside, and the villagers poking around in the embers discovered a new delicacy. This eventually led to a rash of house fires. The moral of the story is: when you do not understand how the pig gets cooked, you have to burn a whole house down every time you want a roast pork dinner. (Rosabeth Moss Kanter)

Understanding what really gives you the outcomes that you want, and what is 'collateral damage' in your business, is seriously important. The portfolio analysis helps you to organize your thinking so that you can achieve this. This analysis is a 'golden oldie' in the world of strategic tools. A number of academics turn their nose up at it – but it is a great way to categorize your products/services and it builds on the lifecycle analysis and the market future analysis.

The portfolio analysis involves identifying which of four sets of characteristics best describe a product or a customer, so you can place the results of this analysis in a four-box quadrant, like Figure 9.4. I will explain the concepts using products/services. The four options are: cash cows, stars, dogs and unknown.

FIGURE 9.4   Portfolio analysis matrix

Cash cow	Star
?	Dog

Cash cows

These are the established products/services that are reliably producing desirable outcomes. The cash cows are those products that predictably pump money into your organization, which can be used to pay today's bills and fund your investments tomorrow. The art is to gently peel away the costs from the cash cows so they provide the highest levels of profit possible.

Stars

It is unlikely that your cash cows will continue to produce profits indefinitely. Therefore you need a crop of new products that will grow into the cash cows of the future. These are the stars. They often attract the brightest people, and they work with bigger budgets and lower profit expectations.

Dogs

These are the products/services that soak up more time and resources than they are worth. They may be the old cash cows that no longer produce good profits, they may be stars that failed, or they may be some kind of senior manager's 'hobby'. They could represent up to 15 per cent of all the products/services in your organization. They need to be put down.

Unknown

This heading is for the products/services no one understands well enough to categorize. They are absorbing time and resources, and may/may not be producing some kind of income. However, until you know where they truly fit, you will not know how best to manage them. These need to be carefully examined, and then properly allocated.

The headings can be applied to customers. You will have customers who are relatively loyal, who consistently buy a broad range of products and who favour your organization. Their predictability means you can refine your processes to satisfy their needs, and the repeat nature of the work means you can allocate your competent people, and save the best and brightest individuals for other, more challenging customers. You should never under-service a cash cow, but there is no need to over-service either. You will have star customers who deserve more attention, and who may require more special attention and customization. You will also have dogs and question marks.

How to use it with a group

Begin by drawing the quadrant and explaining what each box represents. Now you can ask the executive team to perform the analysis. Divide the executive team into two groups. One group will complete the analysis for customers, the other will apply the framework to products/services. Explain that this builds on the market and lifecycle analyses, and forces the decision about where you should channel and withdraw resources.

Ask them to record their completed quadrants on flipchart paper. When each group has allocated customers/markets or products/services to the right quadrants, ask each group to answer the following questions:

- What products do we stay with, and where should we stop wasting our money?
- Which products deserve investment, and which should now be providing profits?
- Which customers represent the best way to fund the business today?
- Which customers will sustain the business in the future?
- Which customers should we try and donate to the competition?

Ask them to highlight/circle the products/customers on charts to indicate their answers, and give them different colours for the different questions. Ask them to stick the flipchart paper on the wall.

You have just made some difficult decisions in a painless way.

SWOT analysis

Overview of the technique

No strategic retreat would be complete without the good old SWOT. The strengths, weaknesses, opportunities and threats framework is the most commonly used way to analyse organizations: so commonly used that in many cases it is treated as a quick exercise that is jumbled among many other techniques and is only allocated a short period of time. When you treat the SWOT like this, it yields poor data. Often the same items appear as both strengths and weaknesses, and sometimes items appear in all categories. This is a tragic waste of a powerful technique. In this workshop you are going to use SWOT to generate some key decisions.

SWOT, like any of the other techniques, is a way to organize the facts you have so you can make sense of the data and see the implications for your organization. The SWOT categories are strengths, weaknesses, opportunities and threats. These are typically placed in a quadrant, as shown in Figure 9.5.

FIGURE 9.5   SWOT analysis

Strengths	Weaknesses
Opportunities	Threats

Strengths and weaknesses

These relate to the situation within your business. Strengths are anything that you have or do that helps you to be successful. Strengths could be a computer system, a specific block of knowledge, a particular process that performs well, your financial position, and so on. Weaknesses are anything that you do not have or cannot do that has the effect of standing in the way of the success of your business.

Opportunities and threats

Opportunities and threats reside outside your organization. Opportunities are any kind of favourable situation that you could use to achieve successful outcomes for your business. These could be the emergence of new markets, the increasing demand for certain kinds of products/services, the collapse of a competitor, the relaxation or the imposition of regulations, and so on. Threats are changes in external circumstances that may have a detrimental effect on your business.

How to use it with a group

You should begin by telling the group that they will find the data they need in the hallmarks of success analysis, culture analysis, skills/talent analysis, financial performance analysis, process performance analysis, risk analysis, cause and effect analysis, resources versus outcomes analysis, relative data analysis, absolute scale analysis and the change readiness analysis. You should also ask them to look at the analyses you have completed so far in the workshop.

Deal with the strengths and weaknesses first. Explain that the first task is to identify what represents a strength – something you do as well as you need to be successful, and what represents a weakness – those things that you do not do as well as you should, and which hold you back.

Now lead a discussion with the executive team and create two lists on two different pieces of flipchart paper – one for strengths and one for weaknesses. Make absolutely sure you gather precise strengths or weaknesses. A strength like 'We have good processes' tells you nothing, while a more specific version: 'Our counter processes mean that we can provide faster, cheaper, more satisfying experiences for our customers' is a lot more useful.

Break the executive team into two groups and ask each group to work on a list. Halfway through the exercise swap 50 per cent of each group (this gives them the chance to mix ideas and import thinking from the other group). If an item does not seem to fit into the category, the executive group should debate this until it is resolved.

Once all the data is properly allocated under each of the two headings, the lists need to be reduced. This is achieved by asking the group to place the strengths/weaknesses into three bands, A, B and C.

Considering the strengths first. Those in the A band represent the strengths that are both significant to future performance and where you have a real and clear advantage. In the B band are the lesser strengths, which carry less strategic weight. In the C band are all the others. If there are more than 25 per cent of the strengths in the A band, be more ruthless.

Do the same for the weaknesses, with the A band representing the greatest weaknesses that will have the largest impact on future performance. In the B band are those that have an impact but are manageable, and in C are the rest. Again, make sure that no more than 25 per cent of the weaknesses appear in the A band.

For the moment, put aside the B and C categories. There will be plenty to do simply addressing the As. Record this on flipchart paper and stick this strengths and weaknesses information on the wall.

Now progress through a similar process for the opportunities and threats. You will need the data from the customer analysis, competitor analysis, environmental analysis, hallmarks of success analysis, barriers to entry analysis, availability analysis, financial performance analysis, risk analysis, relative data analysis, absolute scale analysis, market future analysis, portfolio analysis and lifecycle analysis.

The opportunities and threats relate to what is happening outside your organization. Here you will consider where the opportunities lie in the marketplace, and what is preventing you from taking advantage of those opportunities. Once again split the executive team into two groups and reduce the list by using the A, B and C bands. Stick this information on the wall on flipchart paper.

Take a moment to look at the SWOT information. You can see the strengths that need to be built on and the weaknesses that are holding you back. You can see the places where you will achieve success, and the hurdles you have to jump. You may be tempted to start to define and allocate change programmes. It is nearly time to do this – but be patient.

Concentration of effort analysis

Overview of the technique

> The smorgasbord was just sensational. Hogarth piled his plate so high that little morsels plopped on to the floor on the journey back to his table.
>
> The first mouthfuls were delicious. He gulped them down, anxious to get another helping. Halfway through he started to get stomach pains – but he forced himself to ignore them. Three-quarters of the way through he stopped eating. He knew he wasn't going to finish his plate.

There is one big mistake that accounts for most of the failures of strategic planning exercises. It is incredibly easy to make. It is the mistake of trying to do too much.

When all the problems are made obvious and when all the opportunities are temptingly clear, people want to change their organization – all of it. At this moment a kind of madness takes over and people forget that they already have in-trays full of urgent stuff, they are already overworked, and it is not physically possible to accommodate a large number of extra projects. Too many strategic planning exercises result in 100 projects allocated to 50 project teams that meet enthusiastically for a couple of months – and then fizzle out.

The only way to get strategic projects to take shape, sustain and then deliver is to concentrate effort on those projects that will have the greatest impact, and will serve as a launching pad for other changes.

No more than 20 per cent of the possible 'high priority' projects are going to be able to be advanced. The art is to select the right 20 per cent. To find the best place to concentrate your effort, you need to place your options within a broad context. You are now going to ask some of the big strategic questions.

You have the data and information to resolve them all, but you need to be sure you stay with the facts, and you give everyone enough time to have their say, and enough space to digest the consequences of their decisions.

How to use it with a group

You should begin by explaining that you have so far held off from wrestling with these kinds of questions because you wanted to list and explore all the information about current and future markets/customers, and current and future products/services. Now this is stuck up around the walls it is time to make some decisions about where the investment of effort will be repaid by the greatest rewards.

Explain that you will now consider these questions, each of which will fill their own flipchart page:

- Where are we going?
- Where do we want to be going?
- What business are we now?
- What business do we want to be?
- What is our uniqueness?
- What is our mission and vision?

TABLE 9.2 Concentration of effort analysis

Where are we going?	Where do we want to be going?	What business are we now?
What business do we want to be?	What is our uniqueness?	What is our strategic intent?

As you facilitate this section, make sure that you do not rush. People need time to assimilate the information they have, and need to be comfortable with the conclusions they are reaching.

Begin by writing the first question at the top of a flipchart sheet.

Where are we going?

Ask the group to look at the analyses they have completed so far. Ask them to look at the scenario options analysis, the lifecycle and market analyses. Ask them to look at the SWOT. Ask them to review the information that you have gathered before this workshop. Now ask them 'What path are we on as an organization?'

Summarize their answers on the sheet, and talk through any differences in perception, using the data to make sure that the discussion remains fact based. Stick this piece of paper on the wall, and write another question on another sheet: 'Will this path deliver the financial outcomes that we require?'

In particular look at the market future analysis. Calculate with the group how much you are likely to make if the market opportunities follow your predictions. Whether or not it is enough, you still need to ask the following two questions, which have their own piece of flipchart paper: 'Does this path make the most of our strengths and optimize our opportunities?' and 'Is this path pitted with weaknesses and threats?'

Look at the SWOT analysis. Create a scale to express the answers, with 10 meaning that the path is fully supported by strengths, and 1 meaning that your strengths are irrelevant to the future. Scores on the rest of the scale reflect how successfully your strengths deliver your future.

Complete a similar exercise with the weaknesses. The scale in this case is 10 if your path is indeed pitted with weaknesses and threats, and 1 if it is free of these impediments. Now ask a crunch question: 'Are we travelling down the right path?'

Often the answer to this question is obvious in the light of the information you have generated. If it is not, ask the executives in the room to agree on a percentage figure on how close you are to being on the right path (100 – 1 per cent). You might want to ask each person in the room to independently write down their percentage, and then you can collect them up and write down the average. You are now ready to consider the next question.

Where do we want to be going?

If you are travelling down the right path this question will be relatively easy to answer. If not, you will need to spend some time looking at the information you have about your potential customers and working out how to convert this potential into reality.

You are going to lead the group through some of the questions and thinking that you covered in Chapter 1. Earlier these questions helped you to frame the kind of organization you are today. Use similar questions again to reframe the kind of organization you need to be tomorrow. Ask the group the following questions.

What business are we now?

Make everyone look at the information on the walls. They are not allowed to use any of the labels that are typically associated with your business.

Break them into small groups and give them 15 minutes to describe the kind of organization you are today. Ask them to include references to the following:

- profitability;
- customer relationships;
- people strengths;
- the effectiveness of processes; and
- comparisons with others.

This can be a chilling description. Ask them to express this as a brief written statement. Discuss the similarities and differences between the groups and create a single statement that captures these. This is a bit of a repeat of what you have just completed, but it is a necessary springboard for the next question.

What business do we want to be?

Ask the executive team to imagine they have the opportunity to start again, but without breaking free from the unchangeable restrictions. Ask them to consider the strengths and opportunities. Ask them to identify the best version of the organization that is possible in the light of the most likely future scenario. Ask these questions:

1 What represents the greatest chance of success?
2 Where are there opportunities that we could take advantage of, given our strengths?
3 What is the easiest path to the money available?

Ask the executives to get back into their small groups and describe what this organization would be like, using the same reference points as before (profitability, customers, and so on). Again condense the different statements into one.

Now you are going to create some amazing decision making using the most basic tools. Give the group 15 gold stars – no more (they come on sticky sheets in a stationery shop). Ask them to stick the stars on the items on the flipcharts that will make the greatest contribution to the best possible future.

When they have used up their stars, ask them to keep on thinking about the best possible future and consider the following questions: 'What are going to present the greatest internal hurdles?' and 'What will be the most difficult problems we have to conquer outside?'

This time give the group 15 red dots. Ask them to stick the dots on the flipchart items that present the greatest impediments. Take a moment to reflect. The strategic plan is taking shape. It is time to ask another crunch question.

What is our uniqueness?

Take a look at the data you have about customers and competitors. Consider your strengths and any special advantages you have that are interesting to those who buy your products/services. Consider the organization you have decided you need to become. Now ask these questions:

- What is it about this organization that makes us unique?
- Which aspects of that uniqueness are interesting to current or potential customers?
- Which is the one key difference from the customers' point of view?
- What can we do that that our competitors cannot?
- What information do we own that no one else has (including customer databases)?
- What patents, licences or intellectual property do we own that cannot be replicated?
- Do we have any other rights to do business with a particular set of customers?
- What locations do we possess that give a special and natural right to a set of customers?
- What customer relationships do we have that are difficult for others to develop?

Now create a statement about your uniqueness. This is going to be relatively straightforward, given the data that you have. In Chapter 1 you created a one-line statement that you could place on a billboard. Remind yourself of what you did, and ask the group to complete the same exercise. Write this on a flipchart page and stick it on the wall. Then ask the final question that will lead you to defining what you have to do.

What is our mission and vision?

You have recently created/refreshed one of these in terms of mission and values (see previous chapter), and it is time to stick this on the wall.

Now consider the latest batch of wallpaper that you have just produced. Look at the kind of organization that you have described. Look at the direction that you need to follow and consider what you have to do to progress in that direction. Go back to your gold stars and red dots. These are the areas that deserve your attention, because they will deliver you to the future that you deserve. There are a total of 30 stars and dots on the walls. You need to reduce this to 10.

Ask the executive group to use the information you have just generated – particularly the intent and the uniqueness – to prioritize the items marked with a star or a dot into three groups, A, B and C (you have done this kind of analysis before). Keep them working on these categories until there are 10 items in the A category. These are the projects that you will include in the strategic plan.

The activity hedgehog

Overview of the technique

> There is one thing stronger than all the armies in the world; and that is an idea whose time has come. (Anon)

It can be extraordinarily difficult to allocate the right activities to the right people in such a way that everyone receives those tasks that they are best suited to and which fit into their work schedules. This particularly applies to senior managers. This technique creates a self-serve approach to allocating activities so everyone has an input to what he or she gets, and everyone can see what everyone else is doing.

How to use it with a group

Break the executive team into small groups. Take the 10 items on the A list and allocate these to the groups to convert into projects. So, for example, a weakness like 'turnaround time to fix customers' problems' becomes a project such as 'reduce turnaround time to meet customers' needs, and be faster than the industry average', or an opportunity like 'reduce costs and attract new customers through web-enabled systems' becomes a project such as 'develop web-enabled systems to be operational in six months'. You will have 10 projects.

Most managers have no trouble developing these kinds of projects. Now ask the groups to translate projects into activities and to create a list of the key activities that make up each project. Write each one of these activities on a Post-it Note.

Create a flipchart page for each of the projects. Stick the Post-it Notes around the project name, with the first activity above the first letter of the name of the project. Each flipchart page will now resemble a hedgehog (hence the name).

FIGURE 9.6   Activity hedgehog

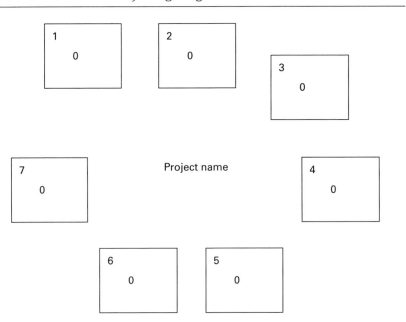

Now code the activities that belong to each project with a coloured dot (a different colour for each project). If you can generate guesstimates about the time required for each activity, record this as well. These collections of Post-it Notes are the end result of all the work completed so far – they are precious.

Let the members of the executive team select the aspects of the project they will commit to delivering. They will do this by collecting the Post-it Notes they will be responsible for actioning. Some managers might want the whole set for a single project, some might want to be involved in some of the design stages of all the projects, some may not have enough spare capacity to be involved in more than a couple of activities.

All the managers will have a handful of Post-it Notes. They should take pieces of flipchart paper, write their names at the top, and stick them on the wall. They can then display the stickers they have chosen on this piece of paper. In this way everyone will know what everyone else has committed to achieving. If any Post-it Notes have not been selected, ask the managers to pick again.

Each project should be allocated an overall leader, and this person carries the additional responsibility for managing the project timetable, milestones and delivery dates. The activities that will deliver your best future now have a sponsor.

By this stage in the retreat those participating have trampled over a lot of data, have completed some important analyses, made some decisions and have projects to progress. A lot has been achieved, but before this group can go home there is one final bit of analysis that needs to be completed.

Movement analysis

Overview of the technique

One of the golden rules for managing a successful change is to 'begin with the end in mind'.

The movement analysis shows the likely effects of the strategic projects on the top 10 business indicators. Profits should go up, numbers of customers in specific segments should change, margins will be different, and so on. These are the movements that will result from the strategic process.

These movements can be recorded on a chart, like the one in Figure 9.7, with the best guesses of the likely magnitude of the change and when it will occur. This provides a yardstick to measure the success of the plan.

How to use it with a group

Pick no more than 10 key indicators that will be affected and ask the group how each one will be affected as a result of the decisions that have been made.

Break the executive team into smaller groups and give each group an equal number of indicators. Ask each group to draw a calendar starting from next month and extending for two years. Ask the group to specify how much the indicators will be affected, and roughly in which month.

While each group is working you can create a 'master' chart. As the groups complete their analysis collect the data and draw each indicator over time in a different colour. You now have an overall roadmap for the changes that your organization will experience. You have also created a realistic answer to the big question: 'What is possible for this business?'

FIGURE 9.7   Movement analysis

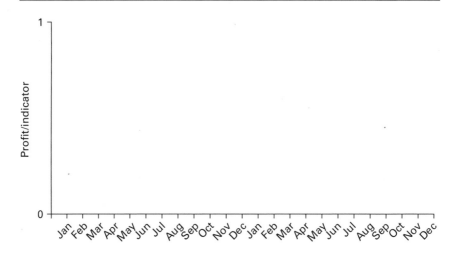

Well done. You have helped your senior people make difficult choices, and you have run a workshop that has resulted in a set of decisions that will deliver a brighter future. Isn't it easy to make decisions when the data points the way, and the questions make the right answers obvious?

In a couple of weeks you will all be together again to do some action planning. This is covered in the next chapter.

My 40-minute video on the Kogan Page website describes how to use the eight techniques at a strategic retreat; see: **www.koganpage.com/editions/ the-strategic-planning-workbook/9780749465001**

Making strategy happen

10

How to lead your business to success

> Grant me the serenity to accept the things I cannot change
>   The courage to change the things I can
>   And the wisdom to know the difference.
>
> (Reinhold Niebuhr)

You now know what to do. You can see the opportunities. You know that you need to move quickly and decisively to shed low-value activities. You know how to use the liberated capacity to generate more profit. You know what changes will deliver the future that your organization deserves.

However, there is an ocean of difference between knowing and doing. This part of the book is about translating ideas into action. I will cover two areas: uniting themes and the action workshop.

Uniting themes

You have built your strategy on the foundations of good data and solid facts. These have pointed you to where the opportunities lie, and have shown you how you can achieve the best possible future for your organization.

On top of these foundations you have developed activities out of analysis and interpretation. You have applied decision-making processes and have selected the best way to apply your people and resources so that you will be successful in the future. You have a robust and practical strategic plan. The senior managers who developed this plan at the decision-making workshop understand how this plan translates into 10 projects, and what these projects are collectively intended to achieve.

The trouble is that no one else has this overall picture. To everyone else in your organization the strategic plan will look like 10 projects. Nothing more. People will not necessarily be able to relate what they do every day to each of the projects. Since your organization is the sum total of all the actions completed by all the people – and most of them were not at the strategic workshop – you need a powerful way to connect what the executive did over two days into sustainable changes in everyday decisions and outcomes.

You need a unifying theme for the projects so that they can be explained, and to influence people's routine choices and decisions. Unifying themes will not change your direction, but they will convert a lot of complex decisions made by a few people into a message that can be understood by all.

The place to look for unifying themes is generic strategy. Generic strategies have been designed to apply to many different forms of organizations. Some strategic planning practitioners choose the generic strategy right at the beginning of the strategic planning process. The only real trick is to pick the right one – and this is where a lot of organizations have come unstuck. There are two problems with applying generic strategies too early: first, historical positioning, and second, it is not a strict either/or choice.

Historical positioning

The average organization has developed over time. This development has been shaped by thousands of good decisions (and a few bad ones) made in response to opportunities. There have been thousands of other decisions less helpful to the organization that resulted in missed advantages and process failures. The cumulative effect of all these decisions means the average business has a great amount of trouble identifying where it sits now in relation to a generic strategic model, and where it should be in the future.

It is not a strict either/or choice

For many organizations there is not a pure application of one choice. For some segments one generic strategy is the best choice; for other segments the opposite applies. For a number of organizations there is no hard rule that governs every part of the business, but rather a broad direction that describes the general intent.

Selecting a generic strategy at the beginning is difficult. However, once you have developed the data and identified the projects, applying a generic strategy as a unifying theme at the end is particularly useful. Traditional generic strategists find this approach heresy, but it works.

In this section of the book I overview four key generic strategies. I pose some questions that you should consider, and give you some exercises to complete so that you can apply the right one/combination to your organization. I cover the following:

- cost versus differentiation;
- customer driven;
- competitor driven; and
- internal process driven.

Generic strategies

Cost versus differentiation

The hotel was right across the road from the backpackers' hostel. Watch someone walk down the road and you could guess which one he or she would turn into – and be right 80 per cent of the time. The most obvious difference was price. How did the hostel manage to charge that little in the centre of the city? By coincidence the owners of the hotel and hostel lived in the same street. Another coincidence was that they made almost identical amounts from their businesses.

Cost versus differentiation is perhaps the most famous and widely used generic strategy. Essentially there are two choices. You can strip out the costs involved in doing business so that you can charge less than your main competitors and still enjoy good profits, or you can arrange your organization so that its delivery mechanisms/products/services are different from your competitors – and valued by your customers – in a way that enables you to charge a higher price. This differentiation can come from the nature of the product/service, from the information you have about your customers, the way that your product is presented and the way it is distributed and so on. These two choices can be summarized in the following two questions. Are you able to reduce the costs of your products/services so they are below those of your competitors while at the same time matching the key elements the customer values, and maintaining your margin? Or do you have unique attributes customers value that enable you to charge a premium for your products/services, while not incurring costs that erode your margin?

If the cost route is the best choice, your organization needs to squeeze out all the costs and gain the most from technology, economies of scale, global labour prices, and so on. If differentiation is the right way to go, your customers need to be made aware of, and become locked into buying, your product/service; or if differentiation comes from the way you do business (maybe distribution channels) you need to strengthen your capacity to exert control over these features.

The sin that an organization can commit is to be 'stuck in the middle' – which means having no clear choice. If you are not sure which route to follow, you run the risk of discounting where you should be differentiating, while saving where you should be spending.

Take a look at the analyses that you completed in the decision-making workshop. Ask the following two questions. In your strengths and opportunities, are there ways for you to develop some form of differentiation that will not cost you a disproportionate amount of money and which will entitle you to charge more? (If you can see that there are ways to achieve this, note them down.) If there is no readily accessible source of differentiation, are there excessive costs highlighted in the weaknesses and threats part of our analysis? (If so, note these down as well.)

If you are offering clearly differentiated products/services then ask the following two questions. Do the analyses that have been completed so far confirm that the customer appreciates the points of differentiation, and/or are we extracting the price that we should for this? (If there are opportunities to improve, note them down.) Are there ways to further develop the differentiation that has been achieved? (If there are some options, also note these.)

Consider all four questions together, and look at the notes that you have made. Create a brief list of the kinds of actions that are required to take advantage of the opportunities.

Look at the projects that were developed at the strategic retreat. The chances are that most – probably all – of the items on your list are embedded in the existing projects. Take two different highlighters. Use one colour for cost and one for differentiation, and mark those activities that deliver cost advantages or produce differentiation. (You will probably have elements of each – in reality most organizations need to attend to both.) Now you can see where the two different themes are present in your projects, and the dominance of one colour will show you which theme is most important.

The identification of the cost versus differentiation is the first piece of analysis that you need to complete. This theme can be developed independently from the other three, which are about emphasis. They are: customer driven, competitor driven and internal process driven.

These themes are interrelated, and therefore they influence each other. It is unlikely that you will be solely one or the other, but it is probable that the road to success will be achieved by emphasizing one over the other. This can then become the theme you use to focus attention and galvanize action.

Customer driven

> Roy eased himself into his company car. He loved the smell of the leather, the hum of the engine, and cruising on the motorway to the sounds of Willie Nelson. He was visiting his clients today, as he did every day. He had a call pattern that he had developed over the years, and during that time he had made a lot of good friends. So what if they did not buy as much any more? No one at head office seemed to notice.

Take a look at the projects you developed on the strategic retreat. Highlight those projects and activities that relate to acquiring new customers and doing more with – and gaining more from – your existing customers. If you have just highlighted the bulk of the projects, then this is your emphasis.

If you need to be customer driven this may be because you are a relatively new business and you do not have much of a presence, you may be too inwardly focused, or you may be poor at packaging what you do in a way that attracts customers. It is probable that you compete against many organizations in an industry where there is room for many players.

A useful way to bring these projects together is to categorize them in one of three ways that describe the relationship that you have with the customer. This analysis leads you to create precise plans that develop opportunities and business with those customers. The three broad categories are:

1 value acquisition (gaining new customers);

2 value improvement (gaining more from existing customers);

3 value maintenance (keeping your vulnerable existing customers).

Value acquisition

> The name of the customer you should really be doing business with is already in your office. It is in the phone book. You have to ask the right questions so that you pick the right number to call.

Value acquisition is about gaining new customers. It is about creating criteria that make it easy for you to identify which new customers will be most likely to provide profitable orders for your organization, now and into the future.

The concept of value acquisition is made real in a value acquisition plan. A value acquisition plan is a spreadsheet that lists potential new customers, and shows the extent to which they possess the characteristics you require. When you have completed this plan it helps you to concentrate your efforts on the right potential customers (those that will deliver the greatest returns).

In the action workshop you will develop one of these plans. Before you try to help a group to get their heads around how to do this, you will find it immensely useful if you have thought through the concepts yourself.

The first step is to create a list of the possible new customers your organization has identified in the 'potential new customers' analysis. The second step is to specify the characteristics your ideal customers would possess. The list will be different for each organization, but it may include items such as:

- The minimum amount the customer spends with you each year (you probably want a certain amount to make it worth your effort in gaining and servicing this customer).
- The likely price/margin that you will get (you want customers who will pay top dollar for your products/services).
- The kinds of products/services that they are likely to buy (preferably stars and cash cows).
- The likely future of the customer (it is good if they are climbing the growth curve).
- The fact that you already have some connection (so getting the first order will not be too hard, or too expensive).
- The capacity of these customers to open the door to enable you to gain other customers.

Now create a table so that the potential customers appear in the first column and there are sufficient columns for all the criteria that you created, plus one for some comments. An example is shown in Table 10.1.

Next create a rating scale. A score of 1 means that the customer has the desired characteristic to the greatest possible extent, 3 means that it has some of this characteristic, and 5 means that it does not possess this characteristic at all. The scores of 2 and 4 can be used to give a little texture to your evaluations.

TABLE 10.1   Example of a value acquisition table

	Minimum spend	Margin required	Key products	Likely future	Entry point	Referral source	Comment
Customer A							
Customer B							
Customer C							

Using the scale, rate a sample of customers on each of the criteria. This analysis shows which customers best meet the criteria, and it helps you to prioritize which new business you should attempt to win first.

You have just completed the thinking on your own. You now have a way to evaluate where you are most likely to gain new business.

Keep your criteria and assessment. In the action workshop you should get the executive team to identify the criteria they think your organization should use to identify new customers. Because you have already worked through the concepts you can prompt them by providing some ideas. Make sure the executives not only design the criteria but also test these criteria by applying them to no less than five new customers.

Value improvement

Desmond took Carl for the 'grand tour' around his plant. Desmond was rightfully proud of what he had achieved, and was pleased that he could show the CEO of one of his key suppliers how the new equipment was being used.

Carl was looking more and more troubled. 'What's up?' Desmond finally asked. 'Where did you get all this stuff?' asked Carl in a faltering voice while pointing to an assortment of machines and spares.

'Don't tell me you supply this gear as well?' Desmond was truly surprised. 'We just placed a big order with Jackson's last week for a whole lot more. I wish I had known.'

Value improvement is about gaining more from your existing customers. This could be selling greater quantities of the products/services your customers already buy, or selling them other products/services you provide but which they currently buy from a competitor.

The value improvement plan articulates your value improvement approach. The plan is as follows. For each customer that has been identified as a 'star' or 'cash cow' you need to create a six-column table that has the following headings:

- Customer
- Current value (to your organization, in sales per year)
- Potential value (possible sales value if all the opportunities became reality)
- Likelihood of gaining the potential value (on a 1–5 scale, with 1 = poor, 5 = good)
- Future prospects for this customer (on a 1–5 scale, 1 = poor, 5 = good)
- Future prospects for this industry (again, on the 1–5 scale, 1 = poor, 5 = good)

TABLE 10.2   Value opportunity analysis

Customer	Current value	Potential value	Likelihood of gaining the potential value	Future prospects (customer)	Future prospects (industry)

An example is shown in Table 10.2. For each product/service that each customer buys – or could buy – create a separate set of columns that continue on and which show:

- current value (of sales per year)
- potential in the next 12 months (of sales per year)
- actions required to achieve the potential
- likelihood of success (on a 1–5 scale, with 1= poor, 5 = good)

Go back to all the data you have collected and the outputs from the decision-making workshop. Complete full sets of information for all the customers that have been covered. You can now identify the best way to improve your current levels of business, using a chart like Table 10.3.

TABLE 10.3   Value improvement table

Product/ service	Current value	Potential (in next 12 months)	Actions required	Likelihood of success

Value maintenance

> One day it will happen. One day someone will mix up an order, or lose their temper, or simply forget to do something. It is inevitable; because we are all human and the systems and processes we build have their little imperfections. One day it will happen to a customer whose business you really need. That is the day that your customer will talk to your competitor.

Value maintenance is like value improvement, except that value maintenance applies when you already have the bulk of the customer's business, and the challenge is to protect this business from attack by your competitors.

Value maintenance is expressed in a plan – the value maintenance plan. This plan is summarized on an eight-column table (like Table 10.4) that contains the following information for each customer:

- Customer name
- Current level of business (sales value per year)
- Percentage of the available business that this represents
- Likelihood that this business will go to a competitor in the next 12 months (1 = unlikely, 3 = possible, 5 = probable)
- Percentage of the total business available at risk
- Reason that the customer will move their business to a competitor
- Most likely tactic that a competitor will use to gain that business
- Retention strategy

You obviously do not need a value maintenance strategy for every customer. Where you are at risk, complete the chart.

TABLE 10.4   Value maintenance table

Customer	Current sales	% of potential	Likelihood of loss	% at risk	Reason for loss	Key competitor tactic	Retention strategy

Competitor driven

There are some industries where the driving force is the constant battle to stay one step ahead of the competition. These are typically the kinds of industries where there are few competitors, low levels of loyalty, and products that are not strongly differentiated in the customer's mind. The challenges are to create a way to get the customer to identify with your organization over your competitors (branding), to keep them coming back (loyalty programmes and lock-out mechanisms), and to keep your organization constantly on their mind (saturation advertising).

Take a look at the projects you created at the decision-making workshop. Highlight those activities that are centred on defeating your competitors. If destroying the competition figures at the top of the list for your organization, then synthesize all the data and decisions that have been made so far and use 'the path of least resistance quadrant'.

The path of least resistance quadrant

This quadrant shows you how to concentrate your efforts and attention. Information can be organization-wide or competitor-specific, depending on the level of analysis that you want to complete. I suggest that you start with the whole organization, and continue to develop this for each major group of competitors and then each key competitor. The two scales are impact and ease.

Impact

Categorize your possible projects/products/services into two groups: those that will have a significant impact, and those that will have a lesser impact. 'Significant impact' means they will generate good margins, large volumes of orders, or will open the door for you to deliver more of your products/ services.

Ease

Categorize the same projects/products/services by the ease of implementation. Those that are easy will be relatively inexpensive, can be developed quickly and will require no new expertise to maintain from one group. Those that are expensive will take time to develop and require a scarce resource from the other group.

You now have two sets of information, and so you can locate each project/product/service on the quadrant; see Figure 10.1. Those that have a high impact and are also easy should be progressed first.

FIGURE 10.1   Path of least resistance matrix

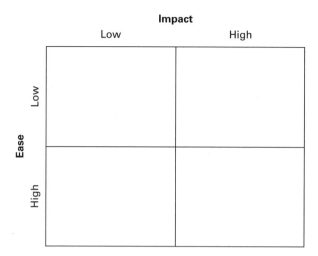

Internal process driven

> Once again, we have managed to snatch defeat out of the jaws of success. (Anon)

Many organizations have all the customers and opportunities they need to be successful. The limiting factor is their capacity to harvest what is available because of barriers of their own making. Their challenge is to convert potential into performance.

Take a look at the projects you have identified so far. Highlight those that are about fixing the internal processes. If the bulk of the items that you have highlighted are about internal processes, this is your strategic theme.

A useful way to summarize these is to use the sub-optimization picture. (You have seen this already, when you completed the process analysis. Here it is again, in Figure 10.2.)

Now you can use it to summarize all the projects. First calculate the effect of the projects (assuming they all deliver what they promise) on your organization. Show what these will do to your standard measures (profit, margin, volumes, waste, rework, and so on). This becomes your statement of the future and you can enter these outcomes against the tallest bar. Define where you are now on the same measures, and write these against the smallest bar.

The next step is to calculate and write down the difference in the middle box, and then write the projects in the 'projects' space. This is a powerful

FIGURE 10.2 The sub-optimization analysis

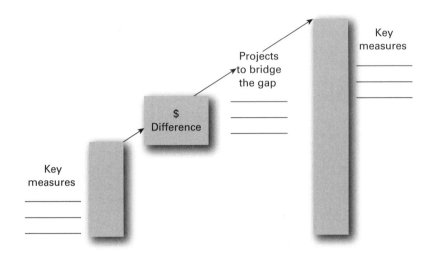

way to summarize what the whole process is about, and you will use this at the action workshop.

You can identify and present the uniting themes that underpin the activities and projects that the executive team selected at the decision-making workshop. You now have some diagrams and tables that summarize your organization's strategic focus, you have built a way to explain what your organization's strategy is all about, and you have a set of terms and titles you can communicate. Soon you are going to bring this together in the action workshop.

The action workshop

Now that the decisions have been made, the task is to create the framework for progressing and completing the activities that will deliver the plan.

It may be that you have enough information from the decision-making workshop to build a comprehensive and clear action plan. It may be that these actions are so obvious and are such a logical extension of what you have already discussed that the executive will have no choice other than to accept and implement them. If this is the case, you could treat the action workshop as optional.

However, if there are complexities that need to be covered, if you want to extend the decision making to a larger group (maybe involve some key managers who will be significantly responsible for implementation), or if you want to make sure that all the executive are 100 per cent on the same page, then you will get a lot of benefit from the action workshop.

The action workshop should take place no more than two or three weeks after the decision-making workshop – while enthusiasm is high and before people start to have their attention diluted by the incessant tide of urgent distractions. A suggested agenda for this workshop appears in the Appendix (see Worksheet 2). This one is a lot more straightforward than that for the decision-making workshop, so I have provided you with more freedom to find your own words and follow your own technique.

There are four areas that need to be covered in this workshop:

1 The uniting theme.
2 The big questions.
3 The change programme.
4 A final check that everything is in place (force field analysis).

The uniting theme

Begin with the uniting theme. Take the executive team through the options available, and show them the analysis that you completed. Then explain how that analysis has resulted in your conclusions about the best uniting theme for your organization.

You now need to translate your thinking into their commitment. The best way to do this is to take them through the exercises that relate to the theme (these have been described earlier in this chapter). Then ask them to list the following:

- the benefits of this theme for the strategy project;
- the benefits for the next strategic planning project;
- the benefits for communication;
- the implications of this theme for the decision-making processes at middle management and supervisory levels, and the key messages for these levels;
- the theme in their own words.

Write all this down, and post it on the wall. This helps (well, forces really) the executive to think through the themes and find their own words to explain them to others. You now have a way to communicate your organization's direction using a simple, straightforward framework.

The big questions

First, go back to Chapter 1 and review your thinking processes.

Remind the executives of the answers they gave to the following questions that were covered in the decision-making workshop:

- What business are we in?
- What business do we want to be in?
- What is our uniqueness?
- What is our strategic intent?

By now you will have 'wordsmithed' what they said, and you can present it all nicely typed and in glorious colour. Make sure that the executive team is completely committed to the description.

Now it is time to bring forward another big question: 'What is important to our success?' Ask the senior executives the following question (without reference to any of your current measures): 'Considering what this organization is all about, in the light of the strategic themes and looking at the projects that will carry us to the future, what do you need to know to be sure that success will be delivered in the future?'

Note down their answers, then divide the group into two. Give each group an equal number of items, and ask them to identify the measures that would need to be in place to provide this information. Ask them to categorize this under five headings:

1 Customer measures.
2 People measures.
3 Financial measures.
4 Process measures.
5 Other measures.

When they have finished, consolidate the lists and tick off the measures that your organization already has, and those that need to be developed. This is an activity that needs to be given to the change teams. (Note: if you have completed the mission, vision, values and measures workshop you will simply need to confirm outcomes.)

The change programme

This workshop is about translating ideas into actions. You want to create the frameworks that will support those actions and choose the people who will complete the detailed work of putting all the sub-steps in place – and that is quite enough for this day.

Before you go to this workshop analyse the 10 projects selected on the previous workshop. Calculate the number of hours that each activity will take, and identify any interrelationships and dependencies (where one part of a project needs to be completed before another project can progress). You can then draw a critical path for each project, and the total programme. Ask the executives to confirm that the timing fits their needs, and ask them to list who they have chosen to be on their change team. Ensure that the people allocated to the change team have enough available hours.

Also before the workshop, ask the executive team to develop a regular review process. They should do this individually for each of the activities they are personally responsible for delivering, and should have a group review to make sure that the whole plan is on track.

You can now present what you have achieved to the group. This will look pretty impressive, and everyone may be tempted to call it a day and go home after lunch. However, there is more. Talk the executive team through the eight key components of change management:

1 a strong mandate;

2 a strong purpose;

3 preparation;

4 the right people;

5 the right action plan;

6 early wins;

7 communication;

8 lock-in.

These are covered in some detail in Chapter 12, but you need this group's ideas and commitment right now.

You have already taken care of the action plan (item 5), so you are going to complete some 'rapid fire' exercises of about 30 minutes each that relate to the other seven components. There is nothing special about the sequence; you can mix it around if you prefer.

Exercise 1: Reinforce the mandate

You need to refer back to the plan that has been developed and ask the question: 'What is going to happen when this is being implemented?' You do not want to dissolve people's enthusiasm and confidence, but neither do you want them to be so starry-eyed that they go into shock when they hit their first bump. (All right, so not many executives get that starry-eyed, but you get the idea.)

Divide the team into three groups. Ask each group to create two columns on a flipchart. Ask one group to imagine the worst consequences that might occur and list them in one column, and then ask them to design a solution for each. Ask another group to do a similar exercise, but now they are imagining the most likely consequences with attendant solutions. Ask the third group to list the best outcomes and what they need to do to sustain these. Together, the results could be shown in a table, like Table 10.5.

TABLE 10.5 Confronting reality

Worst consequences	Solutions	Likely consequences	Solutions	Best outcomes	Ways to sustain these

You have now created an expectation that there will be challenges, and you have also helped the group to see that there are ways to manage whatever comes along. Now ask them, 'Are you ready to confront the reality that there will be some impediments we will have to overcome?' Make sure they have all given a clear commitment to each other that they will see this through to its conclusion.

Exercise 2: Develop a strong purpose

Ask the executive group to see the world through the eyes of the people at different levels in the organization. Break them up into five groups, and allocate each group a different level (front line, supervisors, middle managers, specialists, the top team). Ask each group to list what is important for the people at that level, and what they need to include in the communication package so that it will appeal to those people. Ask them to record their answers – and it may be one of the most eye-opening exercises that your senior people will do in the whole strategic planning process.

You will use these in the written document and the spoken messages, and you will also remind all the senior managers to use these insights as a reference point.

Exercise 3: Make sure that the ground is prepared

Preparation means creating desire and then providing the necessary skills – before any changes are introduced. Desire comes from not only the presence of a good reason to get involved, but also the absence of better reasons for staying the same. Use the time with the executive team to identify the barriers in your business that will get in the way of the strategic plan being achieved. Break the team into five groups and give each one a heading from this list:

TABLE 10.6 Barrier analysis

Barriers:	Impact of the barrier (High, Medium, Low)	Effort required to overcome the barrier (High, Medium, Low)	Priority	Actions required
Process				
Technology				
Physical				
Organizational				
Psychological				

- process barriers;
- technology barriers;
- physical barriers;
- organizational barriers;
- psychological barriers.

Ask them to list the barriers, and their ideas for tearing these down. List them on a chart like Table 10.6.

Exercise 4: Confirm that you have the right people

By this stage in the process the executive team have already thought through who they would like to progress the projects/parts of projects they have promised to deliver. Before these choices are finalized, it is worth confirming that these people will deliver the outcomes required.

Ask the group to list the kinds of characteristics that they think the members of the action team need to possess. These are likely to include items such as:

- credibility within your business;
- knowledge of the topic area;
- interpersonal skills;
- the courage to speak up;
- lateral thinking, and so on.

Create a table that uses these skills as a set of criteria, and list each person who is nominated to be involved in the projects; see Table 10.7. Then create a scale so that 5 means the individual has a lot of this characteristic, 3 means

TABLE 10.7   Change team assessment

Name	Credibility	Knowledge	Interpersonal skills	Courage	Lateral thinking
Person A					
Person B					
Person C					
Person D					

they have a moderate amount, and 1 means this is not their strength. Now ask the group to assess each person using their criteria and this scale. You will quickly see if there are people who should not be confirmed as members of the change team.

Exercise 5: The right action plan

See above.

Exercise 6: Create early wins

This is a quick exercise. Ask the group to identify which high-impact projects – or parts of projects – will be delivered within the next 8 to 12 weeks. If nothing is apparent, ask them to find a way to accelerate some part of what they are doing so they can announce an 'early win'. This is usually straightforward.

TABLE 10.8   Project analysis

Project component	Timing of delivery	Benefit delivered	Estimated value of the benefit	Method of announcement

Exercise 7: Organize the communication timetable

A certain amount of what you have achieved in these exercises relates to aspects of communication. Spend this session agreeing who will be communicating what, and organizing a timetable that meets the diary restrictions of the people in the room.

Exercise 8: Begin the process of lock-in

There are several activities that achieve lock-in. Use your time in the workshop to talk about modelling. This is not about catwalks and skimpy outfits (not unless your executives are particularly into that kind of thing). This is behaviour modelling – which means the executives need to be very, very careful about what they do. If they send a message by their actions – and where they put their attention – that is incongruent with the needs of the strategic plan, you may as well throw the plan away and put the whole process down to a painful learning experience.

Ask the executive team to list the key elements of the plan (this should be straightforward). Divide the team into three groups and give each group a third of the list. Ask each group to specify the behaviours that signal they (the executives) are fully committed to the process and outcomes. Then ask them to identify the behaviours that will imply they are not really serious. Lead a discussion about these behaviours, and ask the executives to police each other.

TABLE 10.9   Modelling the right behaviours

Key element	Reinforcing behaviours	Destructive behaviours

You have now completed the key components of the action workshop. You have made a number of decisions that will become part of the implementation programme, and you have made the senior people keenly aware of what they need to do. However, there is one more activity.

A final check that everything is in place

Before everyone can go home, let's be sure that nothing has been missed. There are several useful techniques that you could use. I suggest the force field analysis.

Consider the plan you have developed, and all the features that are in place to make sure it will be implemented. Now, list the forces in your organization that will help this plan have a smooth passage. Once these are clear, list the forces that will conspire to get in the way of the plan; see Figure 10.3.

Draw a line in the middle of the whiteboard. Draw the forces that hold you back above the line, with an arrow pressing downwards. Draw the forces that will help you below the line with an arrow pushing up.

Ask the executive team to identify ways to maintain the positive forces and minimize the effect of the difficulties. Their analysis and actions can now become part of the change plan.

Well, there it is. Over these three chapters you have made a strategic plan. You have helped your most senior people to make the most profound decisions. You have a detailed plan, and the understanding as well as the commitment to see it through.

As they say, 'the rest is history', except in your case the rest is the future. To reach that future you now need to translate ideas into action.

FIGURE 10.3   Force field analysis

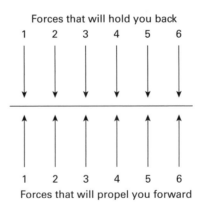

Forces that will hold you back

Forces that will propel you forward

Selling your message

11

Your executive team has travelled through the strategic process. They understand where the ideas and options came from. They know that some possibilities were not pursued and they made the decisions that need to be implemented. They have been on a journey that has developed their commitment, their enthusiasm and their determination to get the chosen outcomes.

The rest of your organization is not on the same page. They need to be infected with the same excitement as your executive team – and quickly. To achieve this you need to write down your message concisely and clearly and you need to present it persuasively and powerfully. In this chapter I will cover 'putting it in writing' and 'show and tell'.

Putting it in writing

There is the story of the professional speaker who travelled for many hours on the kind of aggressively stormy night that only seems possible in the imagination of someone like J K Rowling.

He arrived at a Town Hall to find an ocean of empty chairs, with only a single farmer sitting in the front row. The speaker started to explain that perhaps it wasn't worth going ahead, when the farmer said 'If I go out into the field to feed my stock, and all I find is a single animal – well, I feed it anyway.'

Impressed by this rustic logic the speaker began. Soon his passion for the subject matter took over and he gave one of the finest performances of his career. As he came through his conclusion and finished with an air-punching flourish he was surprised to find that the farmer only gave him a polite handclap.

When the speaker asked what was wrong the farmer replied, 'I said I feed it. I don't empty the whole damned trailer on it.'

The first – and most natural – temptation is to write a large, all-purpose strategic plan. After all, you have enough rolled up flipchart sheets to form the base of a mid-sized tree, you have colour-coded summaries, and you have a detailed action plan. You could write a telephone book-sized document. This would be a big mistake. Not everyone needs to know everything. It may not be a secret, but it will be boringly inappropriate for many of the people who will be on the receiving end, which means that they will not read it.

Unread means irrelevant – and this is not the outcome you want. This means that you need to write different documents for different audiences. You need to create a document that will be used as a reference point for all those who are affected by the strategic plan, and you need to record all your findings so that when you – or someone else – does this again next year the trends and pinpoint changes can be assessed. These audiences are:

- the 'strategic file';
- senior management;
- middle management; and
- the front line.

The strategic file

Strategic planning is a process – not a destination. What is perfect this year may no longer apply in 12 months' time, what seems like a good market may fizzle out after a while, what masquerades as a strength may become an Achilles heel, and what looked like a trend may be an aberration.

The more historical data you have, the more likely you are to recognize real trends and detect genuine changes, and so the easier it is to put together the next strategic plan. This means keeping every piece of information you have, and storing it in a way that makes it useful to those who may follow in subsequent years.

The most obvious approach is to type up an enormous report that tabulates, charts and describes everything you have collected. In fact, this kind of report can be so incredibly impressive that you really want other people to see it, and so it is circulated as the strategic plan. As tempting as this might be, it is an urge that must be resisted.

Even those people who say they want all the information do not read large documents. They may even believe they will settle down during a long flight, or on a Sunday afternoon, and happily study every word – but the odds are not good that this will ever happen. Even the most senior managers need a ruthlessly edited version (see next section).

One way to avoid the trap of writing the 'grizzly bear' report (big and scary) is to make the repository of all information more like a file than a report. This will be a database you should scan in any articles or physical documents you used. Each of the 17 tools should become a heading with a summary of the key findings, each of the eight techniques gets the same treatment, and the results of the additional work to create uniting themes and action plans should be called 'Action Planning'. All the physical working papers and interview notes should also be kept in a box – you may never need them, but then you do not know what you might need to refer back to next year. If you don't use them next time they can be destroyed.

Senior management

> The strategic consultant was undoubtedly brilliant. Anyone who had the same barber as Einstein just had to be. He saw interrelationships that others missed, and he had a rare insight into what business was all about. Sure, sometimes he spoke in metaphors that were difficult to understand and sometimes he seemed to be more interested in the riddle than the solution, but you have to cut a genius a little slack.
>
> The report he wrote was, well, it was a little odd. There were cryptic project names and intricate pictures to describe the decisions that had been taken. There was a project plan that looked more like a blueprint for a nuclear reactor. The executive team did not know what to do.

There is a kind of report that is right for your senior management. You have to choose the style that meets their needs.

The chances are that, since you are reading this book, you are one of the senior management team. You already have a reasonable idea about what level of detail your managers are comfortable with, and how much supporting material they like to see to justify the decisions that have been taken. You know if they favour the abstract or the concrete, and you have experience of the kinds of illustrations they enjoy. However, if you are reasonably new to this group, or if you want to put a little more science around how you write the report, then one way to do this is to use a model about how people perceive their world.

A useful model is a variation on the Ned Herrmann 'Brain Dominance' material. In broad terms this model says that there are four different thinking styles. These are as follows.

Type A: Fact-based

An individual with a lot of this style will look for the facts – and for the logic that strings those facts together. As Ned puts it, 'They will favour reducing the complex to the simple, the unclear to the clear, the cumbersome to the efficient.'

Type B: Form-based

This is similar to A, but is more organized, action-oriented and interested in replicating past success. People who naturally gravitate to this style tend to like rules, dependability and predictability. Like A, people with this style do not particularly enjoy emotions and intuition.

Type C: Feelings-based

This is a very different style from A or B. This is the style that revels in emotions and the people dimensions of any situation. People who exhibit lots of the C style talk about mood, atmosphere, attitude and energy levels.

Type D: Future-based

The D style is the visionary. For the D there are no assumptions to restrict thinking, no boundaries to limit possibilities. You may not understand a lot of what a D is talking about, but when you get a glimpse of what he or she is seeing it is probably original; it could also be seriously 'off the wall'.

First consider yourself. Which of these styles are you most like? Your style will heavily influence how you approach the task of documenting the plan. You need to make sure you do not write a report that you think is brilliant but which is borderline incomprehensible to everyone else because your style is different from your audience's. In the choice between writing in a style that you enjoy, or a style that will be read, always pick the latter.

Consider the management team. Is there a dominant style throughout the team? What is going to work best for the majority of those who are responsible for making the largest parts of the plan happen? Once you have selected a style, here are some ideas about how you could construct your report.

Fact-based report

This report needs to provide the evidence in a direct, unambiguous way with clearly drawn conclusions and all the necessary supporting evidence. An outline for a report of this kind might be:

- Executive summary – a tidy summary of the key drivers for change and the actions that have resulted.
- Methodology – the process that was followed and the people who were involved.
- Key findings – this should be no more than 10 pages long, so you need to select the most persuasive facts and charts and then list the other supporting evidence as bullet points.

- Decisions taken – again, this should not be any more than 10 pages and should specify the key decisions and their translation into projects.

- Action planning – this should outline each key project with milestones and deliverables.

Form-based report

This needs to place any changes in a positive light and to provide as much comfort as possible that there are rules to follow and there are clear and tangible steps that can be measured. Suggested contents are:

- Executive summary – an overview of the steps that need to be followed and the measures that keep the changes on track.

- Background – a brief summary of the information that has been generated and the process followed at the strategic workshops.

- Strategic actions – a flow chart of the key processes, with an indication of where current activities and outcomes remain the same and where there will be changes (see Figure 11.1).

- Detailed analysis of changes – an outline of the steps that need to be completed to make the plan a reality. This should show who will do what and by when. This may have to be long and detailed, and you may need to wait for the change teams to complete some of their work to be able to generate all the required information.

FIGURE 11.1   Summary flow chart for the form-based report

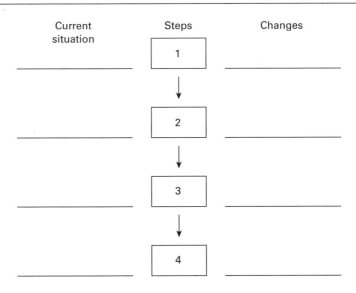

Feelings-based report

This report needs to be less concerned with how decisions were arrived at and more focused on what will happen next. The different areas affected should be specified, with due regard for the people implications. A reasonable table of contents is as follows:

- Executive summary – an overview of the plan with its implications for six key ingredients: people, processes, customers, technology, products and facilities.
- An analysis of each of these six ingredients, and evidence that each will be handled properly and sensitively.
- An action plan for the first six months, which includes a communication strategy.

Future-based report

It is rare to have the D style dominate a group – it usually resides in one or two individuals. However, it may happen in smaller businesses. If yours is like this, you will have the hardest (but shortest) report to write. In this case you need to create a report that is more like a PowerPoint presentation than a traditional strategic plan, with lots of bullet points to summarize key directions. You will also need to create some complex pictures to express where the business is going. A possible table of contents is as follows:

- Executive summary – a key picture with some bullet points.
- Context – a pictorial representation about where the business sits in its market, the key drivers and the forces that are shaping change.
- Five or six quirky headings that capture where the business is going with an outline action plan for each.
- An allocation of responsibilities, key deliverables and a timetable – probably as a colour-coded A3 matrix.

You might like several of these options and there is no reason why you cannot mix and match a little, but make sure that the report you write meets three criteria:

1 it is as short as possible;
2 it meets the readers' needs;
3 it provides no more detail than is necessary (from the readers' point of view).

Now that you have a way to pick the right kind of document, the next task is to write it. It sounds so obvious, but too often the plan lags months behind the strategic decisions. You have probably seen many important projects stall and then stop because they are beyond people's capacity to stay committed to the outcome, and something else has captured their attention along the way. Your planning process is now in this danger zone.

As the author of the plan you should not be responsible for choking the whole strategic process by delaying its appearance. This means starting to write the plan as soon as possible. Depending on the type of report, you can document the key information you have gathered even before the first workshop. Between the workshops you have time to bring the report up to date. This means that you should be able to get the report to the executives within a week or so of the action workshop. If you can deliver it within 24 hours of the conclusion, better still.

Middle management

OK, I am going to generalize a bit here – and what I am about to say will vary from one organization to another – but it is not far from the truth to say that middle managers are primarily concerned with getting things done. While they need a context for their decisions, they are focused on delivering outcomes by due date, within targets and budgets.

Your strategic plan needs to 'talk' to them in a way that fits their reality. This group needs two key outputs from the strategic process: a set of criteria that can be used as a reference point for day-to-day decisions, and a clear statement of what they are expected to achieve.

A set of criteria that can be used as a reference point for day-to-day decisions

The future of any business travels along a pathway of thousands of small decisions. There are decisions that close doors (such as not pursuing an opportunity, or not giving a discount to a new customer) and there are decisions that open doors (such as the investment in new equipment, or the development of new relationships). These decisions shape your future.

Individually these decisions are small enough and routine enough to be made without much discussion or reference to senior managers – even though their cumulative impact on the business is enormous. Typically almost all of these decisions are made by middle managers.

These middle managers need an unambiguous reference point so that they can assess if they are helping the business to take another step towards the future it wants. This means the work you have done on developing uniting themes is particularly important for this group. You should boil down the key messages for the uniting themes and create a one-page set of 'rules' that middle managers can readily apply to their day-to-day decisions. This is a lot harder than it sounds, because ruthless editing to produce a single page is a lot more challenging than recording a jumble of essential and trivial items all mixed together in a long report.

FIGURE 11.2 Example of a one-page summary

My job: As a Partner, I have four jobs (in rank order of importance):
1. Sell work.
2. Manage my profit centre.
3. Develop others.
4. Do work.

This is achieved by:

Profitable work	Profitable practices	New business
I will make sure that for every matter there is the: • right client; • right expectations; • right product; • right rates; • right level of person; • right allocation of time; • right amount of time spent.	I will follow these rules: • Bill every 30 days. • No write-off to exceed 5%. • No fee reversals. • No discounts without a strategic reason. • Collect within 30 days. (The fee earner is responsible for collections.)	I know that the best way to spend my next hour is to sell new work. I will bring this into the firm ASAP by: • putting aside time every week for selling; • making appointments with new clients – every week; • reporting sales activities and sales success; • celebrating the wins with all involved.
Adult to adult relationships I will show that I: • respect people's abilities; • trust their skills; • value their ideas. By: • asking before telling; • listening attentively; • giving (and receiving) praise; • responding to all reasonable requests; • seeking ideas and opinions from everyone.	**Delegation** I will delegate the most possible because I: • analyse what can be delegated; • take the person to the initial meeting and involve them in subsequent discussions and decisions; • tell the client that this person will be doing the work; • focus on outcomes, and let the other person have some freedom.	**A bright future** The result will be: • minimum of 30% pa bottom-line growth in the next 24 months; • reduction of overheads as a proportion of turnover; • expansion of the number of fee earners – particularly solicitors; • development of approaches to reduce the day-to-day need for high-level expertise; • streamlining of all processes; • leveraging of technology; • balancing of work and family commitments.

For example, Figure 11.2 is a one-page summary produced by a law firm. A document like this on all middle managers' desks helps them to understand what priorities they need to allocate, and supports daily decision making.

A clear statement about what they are expected to achieve

This is the point at which strategic plans are translated into business plans. (For those looking for more detail on this process, *The Business Plan*

Workbook by Colin Barrow, Paul Barrow and Robert Brown, published by Kogan Page, provides a comprehensive guide to business planning.)

The key components of a business plan are:

- An overview of the history and position to date.
- References to the research that has been conducted.
- The business strategy, covering the products/services, the market segments, price, promotion, location, channels of distribution and so on.
- Operations, covering the key activities such as manufacturing, purchasing, selling, employing people, insurance and so on.
- Forecast results showing expected volumes and values.
- Business controls that show what measures and measurement systems will be in place.

This operationalization of the strategic projects into business unit activities and outcomes is the work that will be completed by the change agents and teams (see previous chapter). You need to make sure the teams progress quickly so that you can provide a reasonable level of detail, but you should not hold up the communication process because not every one of these details is finalized.

Supervisors and the front line

Too many people give their supervisors and front line a cut and paste of the document that was provided to the executives. It is relatively easy to produce, looks impressive and shows that the executives are really very clever – but what are the chances that it will work? I mean, really work – get the message across in a way that excites and inspires this group of people in your business to follow the dream the executives have created? Not so good.

As mentioned earlier in this book, the view of the business from the front line is like looking at the world from a street-level perspective – lots of noise, traffic and people rushing by. The executive viewpoint is from the windows of the 57th floor – quiet, air-conditioned, and on a larger scale altogether. The strategic message that makes sense to the executives needs to be translated into a gritty reality and a language that connects with the supervisors and the front line.

A really powerful way to do this is to personalize the message. Find a collection of people who will be affected in different ways and then tell their story. So, the plan may be called 'What the Strategic Plan means to YOU'. The document produced may have a couple of key charts and then a series of photos of your employees with an accompanying story for each photo that may sound something like the following.

This is Steve. Those who work at the Liverpool depot know Steve holds the record for eating the most pies at the canteen in one sitting. They also know Steve is a highly experienced driver of our delivery vans, and can find the fastest route through the city – whatever the traffic is like.

So what does this plan mean for Steve? Well, the big change for our business is that we need to get better at keeping the customers that we have, and we need to get a whole lot of new customers as fast as we can. If we can do this we will grow the business – which means better promotion opportunities and bigger bonuses for everyone.

Steve is really important to this new plan because he is one of the people the customers see every day. Steve is one of our many 'reputation makers'. If he treats them right and gives them an experience that is noticeably different from our competitors, then our business will get an even better reputation – and that is a large part of what we all need to achieve our goals.

For Steve – and all the others who drive the vans – this means doing three new things. It means:

- Phoning ahead to the next customer on your list and giving them an accurate time when you will arrive – so that they can get ready.

- If you are delayed, calling all those customers who you know you are going to be late for and giving them an update on your arrival time.

- Making a special point of meeting the people who you deliver to if they are new customers – research shows they really like it if you take a little time to demonstrate that you are interested.

Our business is built on doing these things well. It is people like Steve who make all the difference.

This is something that people can understand and relate to. However, it would be particularly optimistic to believe that writing the actions you want the front line to take and actually changing behaviour will all happen together. There needs to be a deliberate programme of reinforcement and reward. This is covered in the implementation section, in the next chapter.

Show and tell

If you are still with me then you like reading. In fact, you probably like it a lot. For you, reading may be entirely effortless. When you read a novel you probably hardly see the words: they are just the triggers that allow you to conjure up pictures and images in your head, as if you are watching a movie playing in there.

For other people, reading has none of the flow, pleasure or outcome. It is plain hard work. Ask your friends and work colleagues about the articles or business books they have read recently and you will probably be surprised at how little reading goes on in business. The unpleasant fact is that much of what is written in articles/business books is barely browsed.

It does not stop there. Many executive reports are hardly read, executive summaries are only skimmed and most corporate bulletins go straight into the bin. A huge percentage of what gets written for business purposes never gets read – probably as much as 80 per cent is only ever read by the author.

Compounding this is the amount of information that rains down on the average employee. It could easily be around 2 million words and/or numbers every three months. Information about your strategic plan has to compete for reading time, memory space and a place on everyone's daily 'to do' lists. If the strategic messages do not hit their mark, they are not going to be retained.

If you want an important message to get through you need to do more than write it down. You need to talk it through, face-to-face, with those whose attitude/behaviour you want to change. There are two considerations: who delivers the message and how the message is delivered.

Who delivers the message

There are three main choices: the CEO, the heads of the divisions and the immediate managers.

The CEO

Conventional wisdom says that the CEO of the business is the best person to communicate the strategic message – and often he or she is. After all, this is the person who carries the responsibility for making the business produce results, and he or she is typically the person with the most impressive profile in the business. To have this person come and talk to the front line about the future, and to personally explain how that group of people can contribute to the success of the business, is a powerful way to make sure everyone pays attention and that the actions are given a good chance to be seen as a high priority.

If at all possible the CEO should be the person to deliver the message, unless one or both of the following are true: 1) the business is too big, and/ or 2) the CEO lacks 'street credibility'.

The business is too big   CEOs only have so much time available for any one activity. If there are too many places to visit and too many people to talk to, the CEO is simply not going to be able to see everyone. In this case the

CEO needs to make sure that he or she has spoken to the key people who will be taking the message forward.

The CEO lacks 'street credibility' Some CEOs are given difficult assignments. They may have to brutally and rapidly reconfigure or downsize a business, or shake core values, or they may have arrived as part of a hostile merger/takeover. These are the kind of CEOs for whom personal security is a real issue.

If your CEO is one of these you will know it. It is not a secret. He or she will also know that an optimistic strategic message will be treated with suspicion, and a cautious approach will raise the level of fear. If this is the case, think hard about asking the CEO to be the mouthpiece for the plan, because you may do more harm than good.

The heads of divisions

In a big business most employees may be more familiar with their head of division (or region) than the CEO. In a big business where it is impossible for the CEO to complete a road show that will cover everyone, the head of division is a good choice as the person who will present the direction.

The problem is that now different people will be presenting the same message, and may make some minor variations to the emphasis. This can lead to confusion when groups of middle managers get together. If heads of divisions are the key source of spoken information, you need to put together a detailed briefing pack complete with a suggested script and pictures. A good time to distribute the pack is when they get their briefing from the CEO.

The immediate managers

Imagine throwing a brick into a pond, like in Figure 11.3. Where it lands there is a splash, and the beginning of a circle of waves. The ripples immediately begin to advance outwards. A few seconds later the front of the first ripple is some distance from where the brick broke the surface.

This is a good model for understanding who really matters to employees. At the centre is the person him/herself. Next are the person's immediate workmates, then comes his or her immediate supervisor, then that person's immediate supervisor, and so on all the way out to the CEO. This means that immediate managers can have the greatest impact when communicating a message, because they will be there to carry it through to implementation long after the CEO has been whisked away in a limousine.

If you can put immediate managers in a situation where they can accurately and enthusiastically create a context for the strategic plan, as well as explain what the members of their team need to do to make it a reality, then that is the most powerful message of all. However, this is not easy to achieve.

FIGURE 11.3   The impact exerted by different levels of management

It means that each layer of management/supervision needs to be fully briefed by the one above, so they in turn can brief the people who report to them. It means there needs to be a tight 'script' for people to follow so the same message cascades through your business. If the message is critical and there is enough time and budget available, this is a very attractive option.

Giving the message impact

The ideas presented earlier in this chapter about the written report apply equally to the way in which your presentations should be developed. Each group needs a different content and tone. What works for one group will alienate another; what inspires passion within one audience will provoke contempt in another.

Let me offer you some ideas about the style that works for different audiences which you might be able to use for a springboard for your presentations. The audiences covered are: middle managers, supervisors and front line.

Middle managers

Middle managers are used to being the victims of presentations. They can sit for hours and take in huge quantities of information. This does not mean that you have the right to try and bore them into being enthusiastic – they still need to be entertained as well as informed – but it does mean that you can impart a fair amount about the content of the strategic plan. This might sound something like the following.

As you know, the executive team have been having a long, hard look at the business over the past couple of months. We have been away on three different kinds of workshops and we have made some important decisions. Today I am going to let you know what this means for the business, and for you in particular.

Probably the first thing on your minds is, 'Do I still have a job?' Let me assure you that we have more than enough potential in our products and markets to be able to get bigger and more profitable. But we are all going to have to change the way in which we think about what we are doing, and the way we get results.

You know better than anyone else that business has been getting tougher over the past four or five years, and that the past 12 months have presented us with more challenges than we have ever experienced before. Some of our mainstay products do not inspire the excitement they used to, we have new competitors, and we are missing our margin targets more often than we achieve them.

The analysis that we have just completed has made sense of our business in a way that has helped us to see a new pathway to future success. The theme that unites the entire set of projects is that they are all customer driven. That is to say, our internal processes and our comparative position against our competitors are not problems for us – the challenge for us as a business is to get a whole lot better at making sure that every one of our key customers takes every product that we offer, and to make sure that we bring in the right kinds of new customers.

I have used a couple of very important words: 'key customers' and 'right kinds' of new customers. The strategic process has shown us that those we have traditionally thought of as our most important customers are taking us down a path of diminishing returns in shrinking markets.

We have discovered that we do have a clear uniqueness as a business and we have developed a strategic intent that is compatible with that uniqueness, but – and it is a big 'but' – it means that we are going to have to redefine the way we describe the business we are in.

Less than 30 per cent of today's customers are the right kinds of customers for us in the future. To acquire a lot more of these kinds of customers we are going to have to change the way that we win business and deliver value. We are going to have to change the way in which we interact with our customers, and to do that we need to manage our front line differently. We are going to track the progress of this strategic process, as well as our ongoing performance, with a different set of measures.

In a moment I am going to run through the projects and describe the implications of each one, and I am going to give a set of rules to follow. Before I do that, let me say that some of what we need to do is going to be difficult, but I know each one of you is more than capable of making the necessary changes. I know that the real power in this organization is not with us on the executive team – we are too few and spread too thin to make much difference to day-to-day changes. Rather, this power is with you. It is your enthusiasm that animates this business and it is your clear-headed persistence that keeps us on track. I know that you want this business to be the best in our industry and to be world class in the way that we achieve results. Let me show you how we can achieve this ....

Supervisors

It is not uncommon to find that supervisors think people from head office have a very limited appreciation of how the real world works, and they can be sceptical about a planning process that asks them to change the processes they work hard to maintain. This group typically responds well to the chance to participate and interact, and you are probably going to get more connection with/commitment to the strategic plan if you help them to think through the outcomes that you have developed. This kind of process might sound like the following.

> Thank you all for coming. I know that many of you have had to make special arrangements to be here today, and I appreciate it.
>
> I want to talk to you about where the business is going in the future, but first I want to get your ideas about what you think we need to do to make this business really work as well as it should. In particular, I want to talk to you about what we need to do to give our customers the kind of experiences that will keep them coming back, and make them want to recommend us to their friends.

You should have a whiteboard/flipchart/blank overhead project sheet (depending on the size of the audience), and you should start to use it now. What you want to do is form links between what the supervisors say and the strategic projects that you are about to describe.

If you simply ask people to list what needs to be changed you are likely to gets lots of unconnected – and probably narrow – suggestions ('we need to include change of address details on form K72' kind of stuff). So you need to arrange the way that you collect the suggestions so there will be a list of information you can refer to. If you have a set of strategic projects that are about 'customers', create two headings: 'customer-related changes' and 'other changes'. This way you can be sure you will generate material you can use.

> I have two headings here, 'customer-related changes' and 'other changes'. So just call out and let me know what you think we should be doing as a business, and let's start with the customer changes.

You may need to prompt a bit, and make sure that you ask for clarification if you do not understand a suggestion before you write it up. When you have a fair number of ideas – and you can see that you have enough that is related to the projects you are about to present – stop.

> OK, that is probably enough. This is a great list, and I am going to take it with me and give it to the teams responsible for making our strategic plan really work.
>
> You have identified a lot of changes that relate to customers and I want to concentrate on those today. What we found was that the big wins for this business are going to come from treating our customers differently, and getting new customers. Take a look at the kinds of opportunities you have identified today.

Go back to the customer list that you have just generated, and read some out.

> We are all thinking pretty much along the same lines. We have got some projects that formalize these in a way that makes sure they get done, and you are all going to be a big part of what happens. Let me go through the projects...

As you explain the projects, make sure you refer back to the lists of suggestions the supervisors generated, and show where a suggestion is incorporated into a particular action step.

Front line

If you have a reasonably large business there are going to be a lot of front-line people, so you may find that you are talking to large numbers. It is easy for a big audience of people who are not used to business presentations to tune out and not really get the message. There are three techniques used by professional speakers that are worth incorporating in your presentation.

The first is the use of 'pretend involvement'. This is where people feel that they have been involved in a dialogue with you, even though they have not exchanged a single word. One way to achieve this is by asking questions. When you ask a question of people, their brain is conditioned to find an answer, and while this answer is being constructed they are actively thinking about the topic. This feels like they have interacted with you.

The second is storytelling. A story entertains, it brings a point to life – and a story sticks. The third is humour. It is impossible to switch off when someone has just made you laugh. When you put these three together, it might be something like the following.

Let me start by asking you a question. Who thinks that this business is absolutely brilliant, and there is no more that we could do to make it better?

(Indicate you want a show of hands. If you get lots of hands, then smile and say that you want the truth; if you get a few, then say that you agree.)

So, how much better do you think this business could be? Five per cent, 10 per cent, 15 per cent, 20 per cent, more? Think about that for a second. *(Pause.)*

Now give me a show of hands. Who thinks we could be 5 per cent better? *(Pause.)* Who thinks we could be 10 per cent better? *(Pause.)* Who thinks 15 per cent better? *(Pause.)* Who thinks 20 per cent better? *(Pause.)* 25 per cent? *(Pause.)* 30 per cent? *(Pause.)* More than 35 per cent? *(Now pause for a moment or two and look around the room.)*

Who said 25 per cent? Put your hands up again. That is what I think is possible as well. And all those who believe we can do more than that, see me afterwards and tell me what we have to do *(said with a smile)*.

Now let me tell you how we can get this kind of increase. The other day I was visiting Harolds – one of our newer customers who could place a whole lot more orders with us. Bob Reynolds, their purchasing manager, was telling me that we have a great product but it doesn't always arrive when it is supposed to, which means that they have a bunch of contractors hanging about waiting. And he doesn't like that, so sometimes he gives the order to our competitor.

I said to him, 'Bob, we move this stuff by road and it has to pass through two major cities. If it is raining and there are accidents and delays we cannot be held to a perfect delivery time.' He told me a story that really brought it home to me. He told me the story of the two photographers in the jungle.

These two photographers were after a photo of a lion. They had slowly and quietly crept up on this huge lion, making sure that they always kept downwind of the beast. When they got close enough they started to set up their equipment. This was going to be a great shot – probably an award-winning shot.

Suddenly, the wind changed. The lion got their scent. He was on his feet in a flash. He swung his big head around, and his hunter's eyes zeroed in on the trembling photographers.

One of the photographers put down his equipment, and then started to run as fast as he could. 'Don't be stupid,' his friend called out, 'you can't possibly outrun a lion.'

'I don't have to', he called back. 'I only have to outrun – you.'

(Wait for the thunderous laughter to subside before continuing.)

That is what we have to do. We have to be recognizably different from the competition. There are three ways we can do this, and these mean some changes in the way that you do things here. Let me run through these...

As with the report, you may want to mix and match these presentation styles together a bit – but make sure that you do not give the front line the '75 PowerPoint slides in 45 minutes' treatment, or you will definitely lose them.

So the plan is documented and described. The first big step to translating the words into action is complete. It is now time to progress to implementation.

Bringing it all together

12

> I pointed at the moon, but all you saw was my finger.
>
> (African saying)

Here is some bad news. Most change fails. Over 70 per cent of the projects that are designed to create change either fail completely or deliver significantly less than was promised. Your strategic projects are change projects too – they are in danger of suffering the same fate.

So far in this book we have touched on many aspects of the implementation process. In this chapter these are brought together, along with the rest of the ideas that you need to apply. I have been less prescriptive in describing how to run some of the meetings required because issues around implementation are familiar to you already – you grapple with these kinds of challenges every week.

While this chapter appears at this point in the book, you should not wait for all the writing and communicating activities to be complete before starting to work on the actions outlined here. You should be thinking about implementation from the moment you start to make decisions, and I have assumed that you have read this chapter before you have even got to the first workshop.

Obviously, you want your strategic plan to work, so you need to make sure that you are among the successful 30 per cent. To do this you need to make sure that the right elements are in place. There are eight key ingredients that will support change and deliver success. These are:

1 A strong mandate.
2 A strong purpose.
3 Preparation.
4 The right people.
5 The right action plan.

6 Early wins.

7 Communication.

8 Lock-in.

You have seen these headings before in the action workshop. In this chapter I have provided more theory and detail.

A strong mandate

> Fiona was positive the new direction was right for the business; absolutely convinced. It meant making some tough decisions, but she was used to that. Today she had looked at the faces of those who would be reallocated to different sites, and her heart felt heavy. Today she had thought hard about how much of what she was familiar with was being left behind, and her head hurt. Today she worried about raising the money they would need to make this work, and her stomach churned. Today she felt her resolve evaporate, and the first major amendment to the strategic plan was made.

It is easy for people to sit in a room in a comfortable hotel and make decisions about the future of their organization. It is harder to sustain the determination when the first difficulties surface. There will be difficulties. Have no doubt about that. There will be the temptation to dilute the projects so that they become faded versions of themselves – and so will not deliver the required outcomes.

The mandate comes from the CEO and the executive team. You have run a session during the action workshop to make sure the executive team is clear about the implications of the action plan. You have asked them to imagine how hard some of this will be, and on the day of the action workshop you helped them to be prepared to face any difficult consequences, so that they would not surrender to the temptation to back away. You asked them two questions: 'What is going to happen when this is being implemented?' and 'Are you ready to confront the reality that there will be some impediments we will have to overcome?'

You turned the answers into a set of information the executives could use. However, your job continues when the workshop is over and the plans are documented and presented. It has been said that managing change is – in part – about managing courage. This means that you need to quietly but firmly remind the CEO and the executives about the decision-making process that led to the outcomes that you produced.

You need to do this as often as it takes, for as long as is necessary.

A strong purpose

Mark slowly walked to the centre of the stage. He was a magnificent corporate specimen. The newsreader haircut, the crisply ironed shirt, the dazzlingly shiny shoes, the suit that cost more than a small car and the tie that looked like it was beaten from real gold. In his resonant, powerful voice he explained why cutbacks were necessary, why belts would have to be tightened and why everyone had to pitch in to help the business out. This is what the troops want to hear, he thought; this will motivate them. He didn't hear the whisperings in the crowded hall; he didn't know that all they were talking about was the size of his last bonus.

People need a good reason to make a change. Most front-line people do not want to suffer to make the shareholders richer, or the CEO's bonus larger. They need to have a reason that makes sense to them – from their point of view. The 'sackings will continue until morale improves' kind of approach does not work – it never has.

This means packaging the messages so that they relate to how people's jobs will be easier (free of frustrations, or more interesting, or more rewarding), how they will be able to serve customers better (so they spend less time getting yelled at), or how their opportunities to learn and develop will be improved (so they can advance).

When there is a strong personal reason for everyone to make the strategic projects work – then they will work.

Preparation

Have you ever painted a wall? It is not the painting that takes the time, the arduous part is the cleaning, the filling, the application of the masking tape, and so on. It is really tempting to skip all the preparation, ping the lid off the tin, and roll on the paint. It will look great – for about six months.

In the seventh month the grease stains show through, and you will start to be annoyed that the edges are ragged. In the eighth month you will realize that the wall looks worse than it did before. Keep this image in mind because it neatly describes the need for preparing for a change process. Before introducing strategic projects you need to complete two steps: create desire and provide skills.

Create desire

The first part of creating desire is to identify the barriers that will make people resistant to change. List those barriers, using the culture analysis and change readiness analysis as sources of data, and the information produced at the action workshop. Next, get the change team together to specify what needs to be done to reduce the effect of those barriers.

Then ask the same team to identify what you need to do to introduce and stimulate an interest in the change that is coming. Then specify the actions you need to take to maximize the 'stimulation effect.' You have just created a comprehensive set of data that can be added to the whole change programme.

Provide skills

You need to be sure that the barriers and stimulants are being attended to before you start to introduce the skills required – otherwise the training provided will happen in a vacuum and will soon be forgotten. However, make sure that the new skills required are in place just before the next step – the actual implementation of the changes that you need. Work with the change team to make sure that a full training plan is part of the overall implementation approach.

When you prepare the ground in this way, then the change will make sense and it will work.

FIGURE 12.1   Change preparation flow chart

The right people

> 'Follow me', he yelled as he heaved himself over the top of the trench. 'This way, men', he urged as he ducked and weaved through the cratered battlefield. 'Stay close now', he panted as he threw himself behind a low wall.
>
> For the first time he looked around. He was alone. Painfully alone. He could see his men in the distance, staring at him with blank expressions over the top of the trench. This was not a particularly good time to find out he was not the right person for the job.

If you are part of a smaller organization, the team of people who are responsible for working out all the small details that will make it possible to implement the strategic plan will probably be the senior executives. In this case you are stuck with them, and you have to get the best out of this group even though their time and attention is going to be limited.

If you are in a larger organization it is likely that the executives will select some people to work on the details. These are the change team. A good way to think of these people is to consider them to be 'change agents', while the executives are 'change sponsors'.

You will probably have some choice about who will be the change agents, so you should develop selection criteria. In the action workshop you will develop and apply these criteria. You need two key characteristics: the right people on the change team and the people who will do what it takes.

The right people on the change team

Everyone in your executive group is busy. They are probably working around 60 hours a week at the moment. That is already a crazy amount. The strategic projects are going to be juggled along with everything else – and will suffer.

You need to assemble a team of people who can be liberated from their normal duties so that they can do what it takes to advance the projects. They need to be smart, confident enough to speak up if they see a problem, and generally well respected. They are probably the most talented people you identified at the middle layers of your organization in the skills and talent analysis.

The people who will do what it takes

You will already have done most of this thinking when you used the culture, skills and talent and change readiness analyses in the decision-making workshop, and you created criteria and allocated people in the action workshop. However, double-check to make absolutely sure that you have the kind of people who can do what the strategic projects require. If you have people who are worn down by fear, who are worn out by long hours, and who are already working at the limits of their capability, they will not be able to spontaneously 'break the rules to delight a customer'.

It may be that the executives have to make a firm commitment to change their reactions and amend the way they exert power so that the levels of fear and freedom can change.

The right action plan

You are already familiar with writing action plans. You have probably written hundreds in your career. I am not going to try to tell you how to suck eggs in this book. However, it is worth being absolutely sure that you have all the key elements in place. You have already documented each project, including the key steps, and you have created a critical path. You have also produced some key review points, and allocated the responsibility for arriving at those points to specific people.

Test your plan to make sure that it also contains the following: clearly defined end points, a continuous analysis of stimulants and barriers, and triggers for communication.

Clearly defined end points

'We need to provide better customer service', said the CEO. 'We need to provide better customer service', echoed the regional manager. 'We need to provide better customer service', insisted the supervisor. 'But we already provide good service', thought the receptionist – and she kept on doing her job in exactly the same way.

Too many projects suffer from a lack of a clear end point. If you want better service, then what does this mean? What needs to change in terms of process, system or interpersonal response? What will it look like when these changes are achieved – from both the customer's and the employee's point of view? How will you measure the change? When can you stop the project and be sure that you have achieved the change that you wanted? You need to be sure that all these end points are clear, which means that you also need to be clear about what the current situation looks like. Some of this information may exist in the analyses you have already completed.

A continuous analysis of stimulants and barriers

You have already collected this information. You need to be sure that it is incorporated in the plan. However, one analysis is not enough. As the actions take shape and are implemented, you should update your lists and the consequences. Many changes create situations where some people are 'winners' and others are 'losers'. You need to be on the lookout for the reactions of the losers – they can be a source of barriers.

Also, when you make changes to a complex system, the unexpected can happen. The military call this 'the fog of war' and they use this term to describe the effect a real live battle has on even the best plans. You need to be alert for changing circumstances that require you find a different way to achieve the same end point.

Triggers for communication

You have invested a fair amount of effort in communicating the change at the beginning. You need to be sure that the plan keeps the momentum going by developing a list of events that – when they occur – force you to review your communication process.

Early wins

Gordon had been around a long time. He was a survivor. He knew how to play the game. He smiled and nodded when asked to show his support. He pledged his commitment when it was expected. He never let anyone know his thoughts. He would be patient – like a spider at the edge of its web. He would wait until the project started to run into trouble. Then he would pounce.

Any change process has its advocates and its enemies. The enemies are waiting for signs of trouble, looking for the chance to dismantle the change so that everything can go back to the way it was. You can probably think of a few people like Gordon in your organization.

Every change project needs to be able to prove that the decisions that have been made are correct, the sooner the better. It is worth identifying a) what can be progressed quickly and b) what will definitely deliver what is promised. These are the early wins. The executive team should highlight where these lie (see your notes from the action workshop) and a member of the change team should be given special responsibility for delivering early wins. Once these early wins are achieved they should be widely publicized. This will 'take the wind out of the sails' of all the Gordons out there.

Communication

Communication during the change process is typically handled poorly. The senior people put out tedious newsletters that are days behind the rumour mill. People complain that either they are told too little or they are submerged in a blizzard of newsletters and e-mails.

The secret is to find out what people want to know, tell them (preferably have their manager tell them in a group meeting so they have a chance to ask questions), and give them a chance to contribute their thoughts and ideas.

In the action workshop the executives outlined different ways to package messages. You have thought more about this when you put together the initial communication programme. Continue to collect information about what messages are working and what 'hot buttons' are getting the best response. Do this by asking different levels of management what appealed to them and what they thought made the most sense to their teams, and also by asking people at all levels yourself. Use this information to define and shape messages, and make sure that the executives and middle managers know what is having the greatest impact.

This does not mean that you have to run surveys or employ a market research company to conduct focus groups. Simply ask questions around the coffee machine, the photocopier, in the lunchroom and so on. Questions like 'What did you like?', 'What did you understand from the information provided?', 'What made the most sense to you?', 'What would you like to hear more about?' will give you more than enough clues about how to shape the messages, and how often you need to make new information available.

Make sure that you consider all the methods available. It is not that hard to run a short video over your intranet or through an internet supplier. You can have an e-mail 'hot line' for rumours, you can provide key information as a screen saver – there are many ways to get a message across.

Lock-in

The way that things were done in the past is a powerful force. After all, people have spent a long time learning how to make the processes and systems work, they know how to please their boss, they know what to do if something goes wrong, and those who developed them in the first place have a certain amount of ego invested in seeing them continue. Changes need to be locked in, and this is achieved in three ways: behaviour modelling, measures and rewards.

Behaviour modelling

'Customer service,' said the CEO, 'that's our highest priority.' He sighed, and looked crestfallen, 'The trouble is that all the people in the stores just don't get it. I mean, I go there often enough.'

'Tell me what you do', his friend prompted.

'I am really thorough. As I go into the store I do an assessment of the fixtures and fittings, I inspect the stock, I talk to the store manager about casual hours and profits...' The CEO trailed off, and his brow furrowed.

'So, what would the people in the store infer from your behaviour?'

'That stock, profit and all that are important... Oh, I see.'

People do not listen to what senior people say nearly as much as they watch what they do. Everyone in corporate life has seen changes come and go. Some stick, others do not. People want to be sure this one is going to be real before they invest too much in it. The most obvious place to make that assessment is to watch the actions of senior managers. If they say one thing but do another, then everyone can relax and be sure that it will be business as usual. However, if the senior people lead the way with their own behaviour change – then everyone will be much more inclined to follow.

You have gathered some information in the action workshop. You need to use it to help the executives to continue to model the right behaviours.

Measures

Measures focus attention. That is their job. Whatever is measured is put under a spotlight – all the rest is in the shadows. Therefore, institutionalizing the outcomes required by the strategic plan into measures at every level will mean that what needs to happen will actually get done.

This is the most powerful way to lock-in change. The development of measures is part of the work that needs to be completed by the change team.

Rewards

If measuring something makes it important, then rewarding it really gives it priority. Rewards do not have to be put in place forever (they can be used to stimulate a behaviour change) and they do not have to be built into the remuneration system (they can take many forms).

If you are interested in some powerful short-term rewards that will push people to form new habits and will have the effect of locking in the changes that have emanated from the strategic plan, then a good way to make sure these rewards are meaningful is to get the recipients to design them.

So, for example, if you want to reward a change to front-line behaviour, ask a group of front-line people to pick the kinds of goodies they would like to get, within a set of guidelines. You could also ask them to define the rules that dictate the rewards in accordance with a set of criteria.

Now you have a way to transform the strategic plan from a set of documented action plans into a change programme that will be enthusiastically implemented by people in your business. Your strategic journey is just about complete. I have only a little more to add, and that is to share some tricks and traps.

Tricks and traps

13

> Life is like a dog-sled team – if you aren't the lead dog the scenery never changes.
>
> (Inuit saying)

As the leader of your strategic planning exercise, you are going to test some fundamental beliefs you have about how business works. Your expertise is going to be strained to the limit, no matter how good you are. You are also going to be confronted by both conceptual and interpersonal challenges.

I have already offered many different ways to conceptualize and understand how and why your business works – and where it needs to be fixed. This chapter provides you with some of the additional ideas and principles that I find useful, and which help to keep my 'intellectual compass' pointing in the right direction.

It is true to say these are more about tactical-level issues and implementation rather than strategy, but you will probably use all of them during a strategic exercise. I have found that I have been able to stay out in front (and avoid getting lost chasing red herrings and/or being caught up in emotional heat) by avoiding some traps and using some tricks.

I wish that I could pretend that there was some special organizing framework that dictated the priority and content of the items that have been provided, but there is not. Think of it as a collage of material that will help your thought processes. This is not an essential chapter, and if you find it annoying, then skip over it. However, for some people it may provide some very important pointers.

In this chapter I will cover:

- *Tricks:* keeping perspective, keeping a grasp on reality, and seeing the world through others' eyes.
- *Traps:* Finding the solution too soon, following conventional thinking, and not focusing on outcomes.

Trick 1: Keeping perspective

> Two weeks ago Elliott started to get some insights about the business. He thought that he had discovered some fundamental truths. But, now that he had completed more interviews his confidence had evaporated. It seemed that the more he knew, the less certain he became. Now every block of information took him in a different direction. He was seriously confused, and he didn't know how to get back on track.

Earlier in the book I talked about complexity in business. Given that a single game of chess has 10^{108} possible moves, and assuming that your business is considerably more complex than a game of chess, it is very, very easy to 'lose your place' and not be able to properly assess what you are finding or to relate new information to the other bits of data that you have already collected. This is when you need a bit of perspective.

If this is happening to you, then there are two really useful organizing principles to keep in mind: hierarchy and complexity.

Hierarchy

The world is built out of hierarchies. Elements cluster together into small families, small families are subsets of even larger families and these larger ones make up a grander picture. There is an inbuilt order in nature, in the physical world, in technology, in economies, in societies and in processes. This order is always there, ticking away in the background. It will always assert itself given enough time, no matter how deliberately it is subverted by human intervention.

This is why informal communication develops no matter how well formal channels are laid down; it is why organizational structures always operate as a pyramid no matter how they are drawn on a chart; why the front line break rules to amend poorly designed processes so that they will work; why bad businesses eventually go broke; and why political ideologies that ignore fundamental hierarchical human drivers cannot be sustained.

Take a look around your organization for places where a natural hierarchy has been violated, for example:

- The manager who has no natural authority over his or her group. Just watch people find leadership from someone else.
- The disturbance of natural logic so that tasks are set out of sequence. The sequence will be restored.

- A computer system that has been used to define outcomes rather than have the outcomes dictate the system. It will be upgraded, updated, and if this fails, it will be uprooted.

You can probably see some of these in your organization – and the consequences are only too obvious. The hierarchy is the invisible puppeteer pulling the strings. Find the hierarchy and activities/elements start to make sense.

Now that you have the idea, consider any part of the strategic planning process you are going through that is causing you difficulty. Ask the question: 'What hierarchy is at work here?' Often this question alone is enough to shake loose the right kind of insights, but sometimes the answer is not clear.

If you are still stuck, then a straightforward way to identify the hierarchy is to do a low-tech physical sort of the items you have. First list all the issues/items of information/bits of data that are all tangled up. For every item on the list make a card (you could just cut up your list if you like). Find a big space (boardroom table, or the floor) so that you can put those items next to each other that belong together.

Spread out all the cards, and start to push together those that seem to have a natural fit with one another. You will start to form clusters of cards. Once you have a number of clusters, identify the common theme for that cluster, and give it a name that captures that theme. Looking at the theme names only; see if one group has a relationship with another. If so, then put them closer together. Do this again.

Next, consider the relationships between the groupings that you have. Does one set seem to be more important because it drives the others, or because it has a greater effect on outcomes, or because it is particularly important to the direction your business is taking? If so, place this at the top of an imaginary pyramid on your working surface, then pick out the next most important and place them below, and so on. You may only have two levels or you may have more.

Find a straightforward way to verbalize what you are looking at. You have now made sense of what was otherwise confusing, and you can continue to make progress. However, if there are still parts of the puzzle missing, you may need to consider the influence of complexity.

Complexity

The hierarchy analysis will keep your data/decisions in perspective and it will keep you on the track – as long as you have a reasonably complete picture. However, if chunks are missing you may have created information that does not make sense. If you are troubled in this way, you may need to consider if you have underestimated the complexity of the situation.

Underestimating complexity is extremely easy because the dominant approach in business has been to reduce complex systems into their component parts, and then act as if the whole system never existed in the first place. There are many examples of this, such as:

- Processes are pulled apart to form jobs, and so individuals rather than the work system become the focus of attention.

- Problems are seen to be discrete rather than part of a pattern, and so apparently keep on reasserting themselves.

- Businesses are managed as if they exist in isolation, and so market opportunities are missed.

If you are getting stuck it could be that you only have data from a part of the total system, and it cannot stand alone. If you suspect this is happening, you need to try to find the rest of the picture. This is not always easy, but you can generally find enough clues if you look in two places: mathematical representations and interrelationships.

Mathematical representations

Pythagoras – who is known to every school-aged child as the person who proved that 'the square of the hypotenuse is equal to the sum of the square of the other two sides' – was not really a mathematics enthusiast. He was more interested in how the world works. He was convinced that it could be expressed as a set of mathematical formulae.

This thinking is echoed in many management systems that attempt to express complex activities as a set of statistical reports and tables of numbers. Some of these can be very good, and if yours are in this category then complexity will be apparent. However, in many businesses – particularly those that have evolved somewhat piecemeal – the mathematical representations can be too narrow.

If you suspect that your data may be like this, try collecting all the information that your organization uses, and put it together. Again, a big boardroom table or floor is a good-sized surface, and a sample page from each kind of data is enough. Follow the steps that were described for the hierarchy analysis of clustering and sorting. The chances are that the total picture will emerge even though the component parts are stored and perceived as totally independent.

Interrelationships

Sometimes people recognize they are really working on part of a larger process/system – even if they do not express it in that way. These people will often form interdepartmental committees and create all kinds of other formal and informal links. If you seek these out and (once again) put them together, you may find where greater levels of complexity are at work, and when you do, you will have put your activities into the proper perspective.

Trick 2: Keeping a grasp on reality

There are three major obstacles to reality in business from a strategic point of view. They are: imprecise definitions, the tyranny of rhetoric, and too many wardrobes full of the emperor's clothes.

Imprecise definitions

Ask 10 people to independently write down their definition of 'communication', or 'leader', or 'business value', or 'strategy', and the chances are that you are going to get 10 different answers. Many of the terms we use in business every day have no standard meaning and so it can be remarkably difficult to be sure that people are talking about the same reality.

Think very hard about the terms that you are using. Is there any chance at all that you have a different definition from others? Make sure you ask 'What do you mean by that?' You will find the variety in answers particularly interesting.

The tyranny of rhetoric

It can be amazingly tempting to believe that if something is said out loud often enough by senior people then it is true. People might say 'We have empowerment here', or 'Our customers really like our products', or 'We are very sensitive to changes in the marketplace.' Too often these people want to believe these statements, and because everyone is saying the same thing, then it must be right. The fact that there is little proof that any of these are true is overlooked. Make sure that you are not tempted to believe any of this without good evidence – especially if you are a member of the executive team.

Too many wardrobes full of the emperor's clothes

In the nursery story, the emperor was duped into believing that he was fully clothed only to have the ugly fact of his nakedness revealed by a small child who was willing to speak the truth – because this child did not feel compelled to do anything else. In some organizations (and if you have scored 'high' on the fear scale in the culture diagnostic you might be one) there are a thousand subtle messages sent out that let people know that senior managers do not really want bad news – and so their wishes are met. If you suspect that this may be your organization – even to a small extent – then check what is really happening in your business.

Trick 3: Seeing the world through others' eyes

Seeing the world through others' eyes is more hygienic than standing in their shoes, but the concept is the same.

Strategic planning is a mixture of psychological and factual elements – just like any other process design and implementation. The mechanical aspects of collecting the right data and putting it through the right models so that the right outcomes appear will only be translated into action if the psychological processes of creating understanding and overcoming fear are also achieved. The better you understand the people you are working with, the more easily you will be able to integrate what the business needs people to do, and what their 'personalities' will allow them to do. There are two areas that are worth considering: belief systems and thinking styles.

Belief systems

We all live within our own 'logic bubble'. No matter how silly, unproductive or strange someone's behaviour may seem to others, from their point of view it makes sense and it has its own pay-offs. If you can tune into the belief systems of those involved in the strategic process, you are going to find it easier to cater for their psychological needs.

The way into other people's beliefs is to begin with your own, so put aside 10 minutes and write down your beliefs about how the world works. You might find items on your list such as:

- Hard work will be rewarded by success.
- People are only interested in themselves.
- If a deal looks too good to be true, it probably is.
- Life should be fun.
- There is always another way to get the same result, and so on.

Put your beliefs into two lists, one for empowering beliefs and the other for disempowering beliefs. The empowering beliefs are the ones that give you energy, cause you to take action and get you results. The disempowering beliefs limit your possibilities and stand in the way of fulfilling your potential. Next to each belief note down two or three behaviours that result from that belief, and also write down what you typically say to show that you own that belief. You could use Table 13.1.

TABLE 13.1   Belief analysis

	Behaviours	Expressions/sayings
Empowering beliefs		
Disempowering beliefs		

Make sure a reasonable percentage of the behaviours you have listed are in evidence at work.

Now do the same exercise, but in reverse. Note down some of the obvious and most repeated behaviours and sayings of those who you are working with to get the strategic plan developed and implemented. When you have this on paper/screen, infer the empowering and disempowering beliefs that underpin these behaviours and expressions.

If you have key people who are likely to have a belief system that leads them to resist change, to not trust anyone but themselves, and to see life as being about competing with others within your organization (to mention just a few that might get in the way), then you have crystallized some powerful insights. You need to find ways to work around these limitations – particularly during the implementation of the plan.

Thinking styles

The use of thinking styles was explored earlier in this book as a way of deciding how to write the strategic plan. As you were reading that section you may have been thinking of other applications of the model. Well, how about using the same framework to assess the people who are integral to the decision-making and implementation process? To make life just a little easier I have reproduced the key messages from the Ned Herrmann thinking styles.

A. Fact-based thinking style

Individuals with a lot of this style in the way they construct their world will look for the facts and for the logic that strings those facts together. As Ned puts it, 'They will favour reducing the complex to the simple, the unclear to the clear, the cumbersome to the efficient.'

B. Form-based style

This is similar to A, but is more organized, action-oriented and interested in replicating past success. People who naturally gravitate to this style tend to like rules, dependability and predictability. Like A, people with this style do not particularly enjoy emotions and intuition.

C. Feeling-based style

This is a very different style to A or B. This is the style that revels in emotions and the people dimensions of any situation. People who exhibit lots of the C style talk about mood, atmosphere, attitude and energy levels.

D. Future-based style

The future-based style is the visionary. For those with lots of this style in their make-up there are no assumptions to restrict thinking, no boundaries to limit possibilities. You may not understand a lot of what this person is talking about, but when you get a glimpse of what he or she is seeing it is probably original; on occasions it may be seriously 'off the wall'.

As a rough guide, assess the styles by using Table 13.2. List the key people – including yourself – in the first column. You have 100 points for

TABLE 13.2 Style analysis

Name	A	B	C	D

each person to allocate over the four style options. You could give all 100 to one style if that is particularly dominant, or you could spread the points evenly, giving 25 to each style (although this is not that common).

When you have completed this table you will have a clearer picture of how you should approach and communicate with different people, and will also see where there are likely to be conflicts and misperceptions. You will also be aware of your own style and be in a better position to compensate for your own preferences and biases.

Trap 1: Finding the solution too soon

> If the only tool you have is a hammer – then it's amazing how many things look like a nail.

The problem is that once your mind is made up it will search for information that supports its conclusions. It will tend to filter out any evidence that a different answer would be better.

The information-gathering and analysis phases of the strategic process demand that you gain increasingly penetrating insights, but at the same time you do not advance what you have discovered into decisions. Keeping an open mind can be immensely frustrating, particularly if you are used to making dozens of decisions every day to keep a fast-paced business moving.

There is no easy way to avoid falling into this trap. I wish there was. You have to stay aware that it is there right from the start. It is worth asking yourself a key question during all the early work that you are doing: 'Have I solved the problem?' If you have, then force yourself to put your solution to one side and carry on gathering information as if you had not. If you are finding this difficult, spend 10 minutes writing down as many possible causes and solutions that exist, and tick which ones are still viable (even if they are unlikely). This exercise will typically show you that there is more than one solution still available.

Another aspect of this trap is to see many options as 'either/or' rather than appreciating that two or more opportunities can be combined, or be developed next to each other. If you find that you are trying to make 'either/or choices' – stop it.

Trap 2: Following conventional thinking

There are plenty of businesses that followed conventional thinking down a path that led to their decline and demise. These businesses have folded, leaving shareholders, managers and employees wondering what happened. If a business is in a new situation or it needs to create new opportunities, then marching to the same tune as everyone else may not be a winning formula.

Let me give you an example by considering what has happened to the conventional approach to customer service – and why this may no longer fully apply. At the same time I will give you some ideas that you can use to develop a sound customer service strategy.

At the end of the last century the task was to raise the standard of service. The challenge was to redefine businesses so that all those disenchanted customers who were on the sharp end of employee rudeness and process incompetence were able to get a satisfying outcome. The language was about 'delighting customers', 'creating stories' and 'service excellence'.

Businesses that enthusiastically joined the race for superior service are now realizing that high levels of service are very, very expensive. For some businesses the challenge is different. It is now about 'delighting customers, but not at any cost', 'creating stories that set the right expectations', and 'service excellence, but only where it is necessary'.

There needs to be some new thinking, because a good customer service strategy is one that balances your needs to make profits with your customers' needs to get satisfying outcomes from your business. This balancing act is proving to be more complex than originally thought. It is becoming obvious that there is no 'one size fits all' level of service that you can copy and install. What works for a theme park may be irrelevant to your business. What is right for your closest competitor may not work for you. What was perfect for you two years ago may not still work today.

The right level for your business is at the intersection of three variables: customer expectations, desired position and process capability; see Figure 13.1.

Customer expectations (or more accurately needs, wants and expectations) are what you find out about through customer research. Even straightforward techniques like observation, questioning and focus groups will yield a clear picture about what is going on in your customers' heads. The key task is to clearly identify the level of service that your customer expects for every service encounter. You should also specify the two or three aspects of your business that customers really value, and rank order the priority given to all the others. This is the first set of data.

The second set of data relates to your desired position. Your desired position is just that – the place you deliberately choose to occupy. This position is not created in a vacuum. There are three positions that you could occupy

FIGURE 13.1   Finding your service strategy

in relation to your competitors, and you need to analyse your business to decide if you should provide a level of service that is 'the same as', 'better than' or 'not as good as' your competitors'.

You should pick a 'same as' position if you gain no particular advantage by providing better service than your competitors (ie, customers will not select or switch to you on the grounds of service) and spend your money on whatever it is your customers do value. A 'not as good as' position is right if your products, networks, price or other characteristics are considerably stronger than your competitors'. In this case deliver the service aspects that your customers most highly desire, and downscale some of the least valued components of your service package.

If – and only if – you can gain a real and sustainable advantage through having a recognizably superior level of service, and if the costs of providing that service do not outweigh the benefits, should you reach for the 'better than' your competitors' level and invest in extra service features. Having chosen a position, you need to specify what level of performance is required to sustain that position for each key service encounter.

Before you can finalize levels of service there is a third block of data. You need to complete the reality check and find out at what level your processes can perform. This means analysing those processes that directly deliver customer outcomes and identifying the levels of performance that are possible in your business – even on a bad day.

You now have data about customers' expectations and can see what level of service performance is right for your business, and you know what your processes can deliver. When you put this data together, the overall levels of service for each service encounter that you should provide as part of the right service package will become apparent. You will find that you will be able to make savings where you are over-servicing and so do more with less, and you will have a bottom-line rationale for the level of service you provide. Using this model, customer service is transformed from an art into a science, and the basis for delivering service is based on logic – not a slavish following of a conventional position.

Trap 3: Not focusing on outcomes

Your strategic projects should be all about creating the changes that enable your business to achieve its potential. For all kinds of practical, political or logistical reasons it can be tempting to soften your gaze when it comes to some projects and not insist on clear deliverables within defined time frames. This can happen for all kinds of projects, but it occurs more often for projects that are intended to achieve changes to the performance of your human resources, so let me use this as an example. Let me start with an illustrative story.

'So, you want $50,000 to develop the middle management programme?'

Catherine nodded. She didn't trust her voice. She knew that it would betray her anxiety. She knew what the next question would be – and she knew that she did not have the answer that her CEO wanted.

'Tell me which business measures will be affected, by how much and by when.'

Catherine knew that her CEO was looking for a bottom-line return. Instead, she gave what she had: likely effect on turnover, long-term benefits on behaviour and morale, the impact on culture. She wished that she could provide solid numbers. She wished that HR processes and projects could be measured in the same way as the other parts of the organization.

The real danger here is that weak, long-term measures will be used and the project may never deliver the outcome that you need to be successful. There is no reason why HR projects cannot be measured in terms of their real, immediate and obvious effect on the bottom line. You simply need to apply a more ruthless analysis of the reasons for completing the project and more rigorous thinking about how to measure the outcomes. For the HR project (or indeed, any project) ask two powerful questions: 'If this is the solution, what is the problem?' and 'What is the deliverable – where and when will it become evident?'

If this is the solution, what is the problem?

Before we consider the best way to design your project to support the strategic plan, think about some of your current HR projects. Ask yourself the question 'What is the business problem this project is trying to solve?'

Not an easy question. You will probably have to think deeply before you can provide a clear answer. You might find, for example, that your attitude survey is really there to identify if there are problems brewing in parts of the business. It is there to identify future risks. So, call it a 'risk management analysis'.

Now that you have a real purpose for the 'attitude survey' you can make sure that the survey provides an analysis of the risks exposed, the cost impacts of those risks, and the likelihood that they will occur. This is a block of business information that drives plans that have a clear connection to the bottom line. (Is that not a lot more useful than the traditional employee survey, which provided information like, '18 per cent of new employees are disenchanted with the level of communication they receive'? How does that information help you to make money?)

Take culture change as another example. Keep on asking the question until the effect of the change on a bottom-line indicator becomes obvious. Perhaps the outcome is to change customer contact behaviour that will result in a higher rate of cross-selling. If this is the case, you can call it 'the sales improvement project' and get information about cross-selling rates before the project, predict the percentage change that will result from the project (and how long it will be before those changes show up in business measures), and measure again afterwards. If you predict a 15 per cent improvement, which is worth, say, $500,000 per year, then you should be able to demonstrate that your project has delivered this outcome.

This simple question has helped to make a lot of sense of your current projects, and it has shown you how to create obvious measures that enable you to connect the project to the bottom line. Now ask this question as you design your strategic projects. You will have a lot of data to help you to answer this question. Make sure that you make the best possible use of it all. You can then progress to the next question.

What is the deliverable – where and when will it become evident?

The previous question has forced you to identify the true nature and magnitude of the project, and where its impact will be felt. Now all that remains is to specify the time frames. A chart like Table 13.3 forces you to provide the right level of detail. You should be able to produce a chart like this for every project using real business measures.

TABLE 13.3   Identifying clear outcomes

Project	Business measure affected	Current level	Target level	% change	Value of that change (in $)	% in the first 2 months	% in 4 months	% in 6 months	Total cost	Return ratio

So, there are three tricks and three traps. You probably have your own models, principles and guiding frameworks. You will probably use all your accumulated wisdom during the journey towards your strategic plan.

I hope you have enjoyed taking the journey through your business and into your future with me. You will find articles and videos available on my website. They are currently all free: just go to **www.lakegroup.com.au** and help yourself.

Appendix: Worksheets

This book contains diagnostics, frameworks, models, techniques and analysis tools. These are described in the chapters where they are used, and their application is explained in the context of the strategic process.

This Appendix summarizes the key tools that you have used in your strategic process. They are reproduced here, together at the back of the book, so that you can easily find them when you are running the workshops. I have presented them as worksheets.

This Appendix also provides draft agendas for the three workshops, based on how long I have found it takes to cover the topics. You may think that some of the time allocations are too long, but I am willing to bet that you will be grateful if you stick with the periods allowed.

Once you are familiar with these tools and techniques you will find other uses for them. They are all essentially ways to organize information so that the real situation becomes clearer, the options available become more obvious, and the decisions are easier.

May they serve you well.

Worksheet 1: Draft agenda for the decision-making workshop

This draft agenda is intended to be a guide. When you look at the data you have collected you may want to give some areas more/less attention. Just make sure that you cover all the key areas.

This is a two-day workshop. I have concluded each day at around 6 pm, but you can keep going into the night. However, you run the real risk that people will make any decision out of fatigue, which is obviously going to waste the effort that you have invested. If you sense that this is happening at any time, introduce a break. I have also recommended reasonably long morning and afternoon tea breaks.

You should hold this workshop off site. You will find that it works better when the senior people are a long way from interruptions – and their mobile phones are switched off.

Day one

8.30	Introduction. Everyone knows each other, so this is really about getting people relaxed. Maybe ask people to tell the group something that they probably do not know, or to give three facts about themselves only two of which are true (they need to discover the false one over tea, dinner, and so on).
9.00	Expectations. An overview of the programme, the ground rules, CEO's introduction.
9.30	A review of the data. You should overview all the data that has been collected, and point to the key items. You might like to get different people to talk through different items to keep it interesting.
10.30	Morning tea
11.00	The scenario options analysis
12.45	Lunch
1.45	Market future analysis
3.15	Afternoon tea
3.45	Lifecycle analysis
5.00	Portfolio analysis
6.00	Close

Day two

8.30	Recap day one
8.45	Complete portfolio analysis
10.30	Morning tea
11.00	SWOT
12.45	Lunch
1.45	Concentration of effort analysis
3.15	Afternoon tea
3.45	Activity hedgehog
4.45	Movement analysis
5.30	Consolidation of the events of the two days, foreshadow the next workshop
6.00	Close
6.01	A relaxing drink in the bar

Worksheet 2: Draft agenda for the mission, vision and values workshop and the measures workshop

Day one – mission, vision and values

8.30	Introductions and review of the key points from the decision-making workshop
9.00	The vision statement – an overview
9.15	The two questions
9.30	Key word generation in small groups
9.50	First round of consolidation
10.10	Second round of consolidation to produce the agreed set of words
10.30	Morning tea (wordsmiths to work through the tea break)
11.00	The mission statement – an overview
11.15	Review data
11.35	Key word generation in small groups
11.55	First round of consolidation
12.15	Second round of consolidation to produce an agreed set of words
12.35	Lunch (wordsmiths to work through lunch break – but do let them eat something anyway)
1.15	Review of the wordsmithed statements
1.20	Generate lists of key behaviours
2.10	Identify the values that give rise to the behaviours
2.40	Consolidate the values
3.00	Afternoon tea (wordsmiths to work through tea break)
3.20	Review all the statements together
3.45	Discuss implications
4.30	Close

Day two – measures

8.30	Review key points from the mission, vision and values workshop
8.45	The role of measures in the process – an overview
9.00	Generate measures for the mission, vision, values and other categories

10.30	Morning tea
11.00	Allocate the measures to the processes, people, customers and finance categories
11.20	Add to the set of measures so that there is a reasonable representation in each category
12.00	Allocate the measures to the categories: Level 1, Level 2, Level 3, Level 4
12.30	Lunch
1.10	Refine and add to the set of measures so that there is a flow of measures across all levels
2.30	Discuss
2.45	Mark those measures that do not exist and need to be developed
3.00	Afternoon tea
3.15	Discuss reporting implications
4.00	Close

Note: These workshops could be run together as a two-day event, or independently.

Worksheet 3: Draft agenda for the action workshop

This is a one-day workshop. It does not have to be off site.

Morning

8.30	Review of the key points to come out of the decision-making workshop/mission, vision, values and measures workshop
9.00	The four uniting themes
10.30	Morning tea
11.00	The change programme
12.30	Lunch

Afternoon

1.30	The change programme (cont'd)
3.30	Afternoon tea
5.00	The force field analysis
5.30	Conclusion, any final points, CEO's message
5.45	Close

Worksheet 4: The sub-optimization analysis

This is a robust and revealing analysis. It has been used in three places in this book – as a broad framework to consider process performance, as a diagnostic tool to assess the gap between current and possible performance, and as a framework to summarize an internally focused strategic theme.

FIGURE A.1 The sub-optimisation analysis

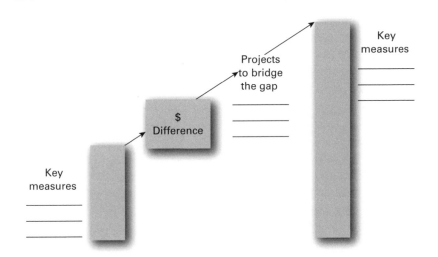

How it works

1 First picture the optimized state. This is where everyone performs at the level of your best worker, every customer is as profitable as your best customer, and all processes are sleek and efficient. This state is represented by the tall bar on the chart. Write down the level of performance you could achieve for your top five key business measures next to this bar.

2 Specify the current state. This is represented by the short bar. Note down what this looks like, using the same five measures.

3 Calculate the difference between being where you are now and where you could be. You should include the extra costs that you are incurring, and the profits that you are sacrificing. Write this in the box in the middle.

4 Specify the projects that will get you from the current to the optimized state. Put at the top of the list those projects that will have the greatest effect, in the shortest amount of time, with the least amount of effort.

What it shows

This is a powerful way to show what your organization could become if the impediments were removed and the opportunities were seized. The size of the difference gap provides the impetus to want to make the required changes; the list of projects shows what needs to be done.

Worksheet 5: Tables

The table is the most versatile way to collect and present complex data. It is a format that most people are familiar with, and that most people can use on their PC. Tables have been used throughout the book.

TABLE A.1   The table

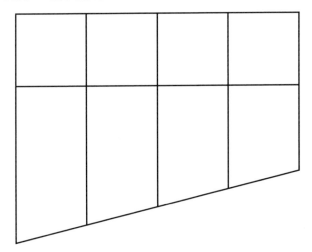

Different numbers of columns have been used for the different types of analysis. These have been explained in the parts of the book where they appear. Some handy hints are as follows:

- Use as few words as possible. People do not mind the boiled down version that delivers meaning; they do mind having to struggle through pages of analysis because too many words stretch the columns.
- Place the most significant data first.
- If there is a lot of data, prepare a one-page summary.
- If you need to, do not be concerned about using an A3 format. You can get a lot of information on the page ... and it looks really important.
- Use a highlighter to pick out key trends.

How they work

Tables are remarkably versatile, easy to present, and relate many different pieces of information. You will see that in many cases you have been asked to highlight parts of the tables to make key information stand out.

What they show

The different tables used in this book provide different information. You need to go back to the chapter where they are first mentioned to identify what data needs to be inserted and what conclusions can be drawn.

Worksheet 6: Hallmarks of success analysis

This is a quick way to gain some penetrating insights. In this analysis you are collecting two pieces of data: the distinguishing features that really make a difference, and how well you perform against those features.

TABLE A.2   The hallmarks of success analysis

Feature	Rank	Current performance	Improvement opportunity

How it works

1 Select a group of people who will provide you with the data you need.
2 Ask them individually to think about what distinguishes those who are truly great (at doing whatever you are investigating).
3 Ask them to identify the top five to six features that deliver this greatness.
4 Ask them to rank order this list.
5 Ask them to give your organization a score for each of these features. (1 means that you have more of this feature than other organizations, 3 means that you have average, 5 means that you have less than the rest.)
6 Ask them to identify the improvements that will produce a score of 1.
7 Consolidate the results from your interviews onto one table, with the most frequently nominated feature at the top of the list, and an average of the scores.

What it shows

This is a revealing look at why your organization is not being as successful as it could be – or should be. It focuses attention on those key features where you need to make improvements.

Worksheet 7: The fear/freedom culture analysis

Corporate culture is a key driver of organizational performance. The fear/freedom analysis is a quick way to reveal some of the key elements of the culture inside your organization.

Fear and freedom are two elements that are present to a greater or lesser extent in all organizations. High or low levels of fear produce predictable behaviours, as do high or low levels of freedom. Combining these on the same scale provides an interesting snapshot of the behaviours you are likely to have in your organization.

FIGURE A.2   Fear–freedom analysis scale

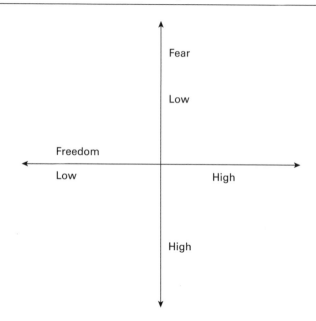

How it works

1 Collect data from focus groups that shows you how much fear is present (see the section in Chapter 3 for the questions).

2 Research the levels of freedom and delegated authority that are conferred and used. Assess the appropriateness by asking if the delegations are sufficient to get the week-to-week work completed without reference to a more senior person. Assess the answers on a scale that shows 'high' freedom (fully responsible and able to make

all necessary decisions), 'medium' (key decisions not available) and 'low' (needs to refer even the most trivial decisions).

3 Assess the degree of fear on a three-point scale – high, medium and low. (High means that people are afraid of making changes, offering ideas or holding a different viewpoint from their manager, and are concerned about losing their job. Low means there is little use of hierarchical power, everyone feels safe to express their views and experiment with new ways to achieve results, and they feel that their jobs are secure. Medium is in between.)

4 Show where your organization fits on the four-quadrant scale.

What it shows

Your position on the quadrant tells you what shared behaviours are likely to be present in your organization:

- Low fear + high freedom = innovative, accepting of change, experimental.
- Low fear + low freedom = frustration, challenges to authority, rules will be broken.
- High fear + high freedom = upward delegation, meetings to share decisions, low innovation.
- High fear + low freedom = dependence on rules and precedents, resistance to change.

Worksheet 8: Resources versus outcomes analysis

This is a straightforward way to assess the outcomes that are delivered by the resources invested.

FIGURE A.3   Resources-outcomes analysis

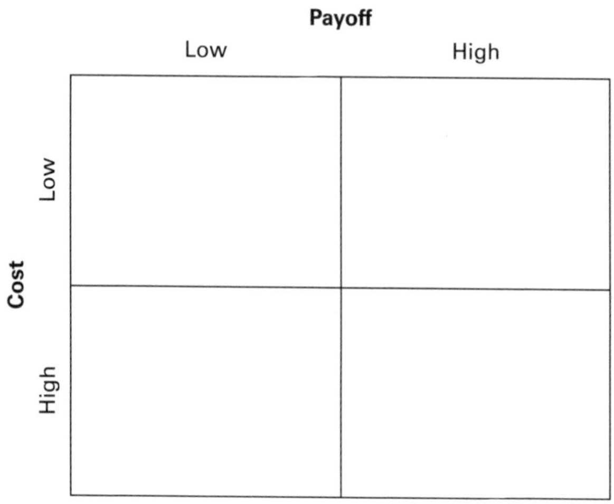

How it works

1 First produce a list of the parts of your organization that consume large quantities of resources.

2 Calculate all the costs associated with running that part of the organization. Include management time, rent, and any hidden costs, along with the salaries, equipment and other resources.

3 List the outcomes and place a monetary value next to each item. This could be expressed as the money saved, or the profits produced/ stimulated, or both.

4 Rank order the costs, and the money returned.

5 Those that represent the top 25 per cent costs should be considered high, those that deliver the top 25 per cent of the outcomes should also be considered high.

6 In a similar way, the bottom 25 per cent for both should be considered low.

7 Place the items on your list in the correct place in the quadrant.

8 The score in between can be placed closer to the midlines of the quadrant.

What it shows

You can see at a glance which items are:

- costing little, but returning a lot;
- costing a lot and returning little;
- costing little, but returning little;
- costing a lot, but returning a lot.

You need to scrutinize the middle two, and review the fourth item.

Worksheet 9: Market future analysis

This is a graphical way to show what is likely to happen in the key markets where you are active. It turns lots of written information into an 'instrument panel' that shows what will probably happen in the future.

FIGURE A.4 Key market analysis

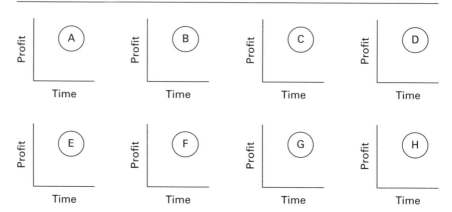

How it works

1 Make a list of the key markets in which you operate, and include any large customers.

2 Create a straightforward graph of time (horizontal axis) and profit (on the vertical axis).

3 Show the profits (or sales if you cannot get profits) for each market/large customer over the past two years, and the projections for the next three years.

4 Draw a line on each graph that represents the past and the estimated future.

5 Put all the graphs next to each other.

What it shows

The direction of the lines is the key:

- If all the lines are heading south, your profits are going to suffer.
- If some areas are in decline, you need to consider if you should continue to be in that market.
- If there are good possibilities in some markets, you should consider investing more effort to take a larger share.

Worksheet 10: Lifecycle analysis

Just about every product, industry and market will go through a lifecycle. Like the human lifecycle, there is the amazing investment of resources at the beginning, the growth spurt in adolescence, the maturing and slowing down, and the decline.

The position on the lifecycle chart determines investment decisions, profit expectations, the way in which controls are allocated, and expectations for the future.

FIGURE A.5   Lifecycle analysis

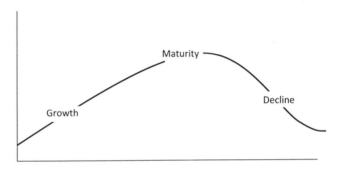

How it works

Allocate your products/services to the stage in the lifecycle that they occupy.

What it shows

This graph shows where the bulk of your products/services are located. If you have most/all in maturity and decline, then you will need to start to develop the next generation.

It also shows if you are investing where you should, and saving where you could.

Worksheet 11: Portfolio analysis

This is a way to force people to allocate products/services (or customers, depending on the subject of the analysis) into different categories. Once in those categories it is easier to make difficult decisions. There are four categories:

1 *Cash cows.* These are the established products/services that reliably produce desirable outcomes. These products predictably pump money into the organization that can be used to pay today's bills and fund your investments tomorrow.

2 *Stars.* It is unlikely that your cash cows will continue to produce profits indefinitely. Therefore you need a crop of new products that will grow into the cash cows of the future. These are the stars.

3 *Dogs.* These are the products/services that soak up more time and resources than they are worth. They might be the old cash cows that no longer produce good profits, they may be stars that failed, or they may be some kind of senior manager's 'hobby'.

4 *Unknown.* This heading is for the products/services that no one understands well enough to categorize. They are absorbing time and resources, and they may/may not be producing some kind of income.

FIGURE A.6 Portfolio analysis matrix

Cash cow	Star
?	Dog

How it works

Using the data available, allocate the products/services to one of the categories. Rank order the items in each category, with the one that is closest to the definition at the top.

What it shows

- If there are too few cash cows, you will probably be starved of funds. You need to convert some stars – quickly.
- If there are too few stars, you have not invested enough in the future – a crunch is on the way.
- If there are any dogs, they should be put down.
- The unknowns need to be carefully examined, and allocated to another category when more data is available.

Worksheet 12: The activity hedgehog

This is a great way to identify the activities that belong to a project, and then allocate these activities to the people who will make them happen.

FIGURE A.7 Activity hedgehog

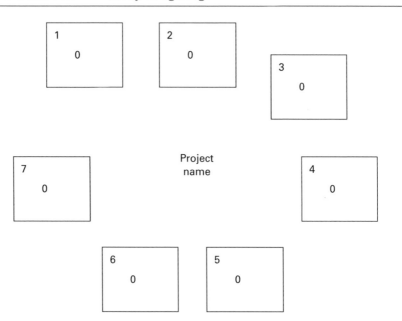

How it works

1 Select the projects that you want to progress.

2 List the activities that deliver each project.

3 Write the project name in the middle of a page, and write the activities that belong to the project on Post-it Notes, one note per activity.

4 Arrange the activities around the name.

5 Colour code the projects, and place a coloured dot on each Post-it Note (so you can easily see which activity goes with each project).

6 Now you can ask a group of people to select which project, or parts of a project, they will deliver.

7 They will select the notes, and stick them on a piece of paper with their name at the top.

What it shows

Allocating responsibility can be remarkably difficult and time-consuming. This approach shows the key activities, who will be responsible for delivering those activities, and how the people involved need to interact.

Worksheet 13: The path of least resistance quadrant

This shows you the easiest way to make the greatest impact. It can be applied to a number of different problems; in this book it has been used to identify the best way to gain an edge over a competitor.

FIGURE A.8   Path of least resistance matrix

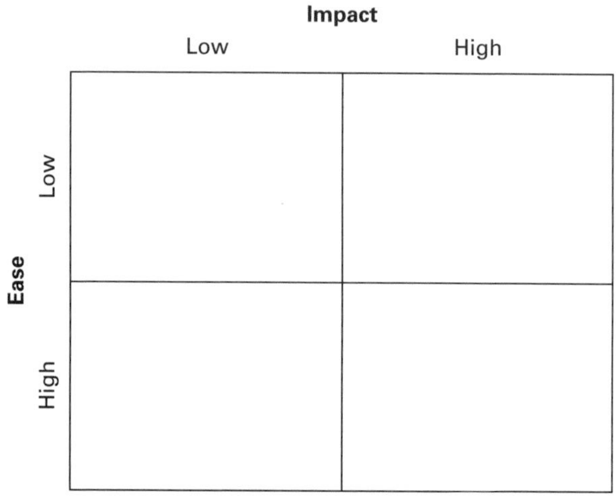

How it works

1 Categorize your products/services into two groups: those that will have a great impact and those that will not. High-impact products/ services deliver good margins, contain large volumes and open the door for you to do more business. Low-impact products/services have the opposite characteristics.

2 Categorize your products and services again, this time into another two groups: those that are easy to implement and those that require significant investment. Those that are easy will cost little, be ready quickly and not require any expertise or equipment that you do not have already. Those that are difficult will have the opposite characteristics.

3 Now position each product/service in the quadrant, using the two pieces of information that you have.

What it shows

- High-impact, high-ease products/services are those that offer the greatest chance of success.
- High-impact, low-ease products/services are going to be slow to deliver, and will not deliver a profit in the short term.
- Low-impact, high-ease products/services may include some quick wins.
- Low-impact, low-ease products/services will probably not be worth the trouble.

Worksheet 14: The change preparation flow chart

Change does not start when a new set of processes to support a strategic project is installed. It does not start when the necessary training is provided. Change starts when people accept that change is coming and are interested in making it work. The preparation flow chart shows the psychological process that precedes the physical changes.

FIGURE A.9 Change preparation flow chart

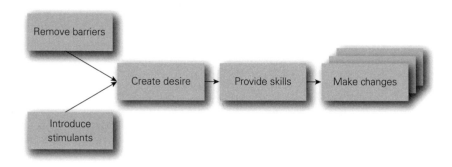

How it works

1 Identify all the attitudes, people, processes and systems that will get in the way of the changes that you want to achieve. These are the barriers.

2 Identify what you could do to get people excited about the change that is coming. These are the stimulants.

3 Develop a plan that will minimize the barriers and maximize the stimulants.

4 Introduce this plan in advance of the training and the physical change. Do not try to make any of the changes happen until you have created 'fertile soil', or they will perish.

5 When people are ready for the changes, provide the training.

What it shows

The likelihood that the change will be accepted, and the actions that will prepare the ground for the change.

Worksheet 15: The force field analysis

This is a quick way to identify what you need to take care of so that the projects will have the smoothest possible journey. It forces a group of people to recognize, and then address, the positive and negative forces that will impact on the activities.

FIGURE A.10   Force field analysis

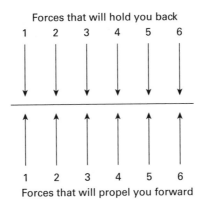

Forces that will hold you back

Forces that will propel you forward

How it works

1 Draw a horizontal line through the middle of a whiteboard.

2 Ask the group to specify the forces that will get in the way of implementing the strategic projects.

3 Enter these above the line, with a downward arrow from each pressing down on the line.

4 Ask the group to identify the forces that will help you to implement the strategic projects.

5 Draw these below the line, with the arrows pushing upwards.

6 Ask the group to identify ways to strengthen the positive forces and weaken the negative.

7 Prioritize these actions, and incorporate them in the overall implementation plan.

What it shows

This analysis foreshadows problems. It also highlights where you can gain support.

INDEX

NB page numbers in *italics* indicate figures or tables